how to choose the wrong marriage partner and live unhappily ever after

ROBERT L. MASON, Jr.

CAROLINE L. JACOBS

John Knox Press
ATLANTA

Library of Congress Cataloging in Publication Data

Mason, Robert Lee.
  How to choose the wrong marriage partner and live
unhappily ever after

  1. Mate selection. 2. Marriage. 3. Divorce.
I. Jacobs, Carrie, 1940-   joint author.
II. Title.
HQ734.M4297   301.42   78-52452
ISBN 0–8042–2093–X pbk.

©copyright 1979 John Knox Press
Atlanta, Georgia
Printed in the United States of America

contents

61779

preface

This book is addressed to those individuals, both young and old, who are thinking of marriage. We are interested in reaching couples before rather than after marriage. Although we are aware that there is no way to predict success or failure in marriage with any great degree of accuracy, our major interest is that of postponing or preventing marriage between individuals who, in the courtship stage, are already showing signs which strongly suggest they will have considerable difficulty making it together. More specifically, our purpose is that of alerting persons in the process of choosing a husband or wife to some of the common differences or problems which most often lead to difficulty in building a lasting and rewarding marriage.

It is our contention that if the couples reported on in the pages of this book had given more attention to their problems and conflicts while dating, many of them would never have experienced the serious problems they encountered after marriage. Many would never have married at all.

While designed primarily for individual use, the book can easily be adapted for use in church study groups, high school classes in psychology and sociology, and college courses in marriage and family. Although not addressed specifically to those already married, this book can be used to alert married couples to problems not yet in the crisis stage. If this is achieved, help can be sought, and it is possible that a major marital catastrophe can be avoided.

Finally, it is hoped that this may be of service to the many men and women, once married but now single due to divorce or death, who hope to remarry.

CHAPTER 1.

divorce

The seventy-three-old courthouse clock had just struck eleven when Jan approached the marble steps leading to the judge's chambers where, in fifteen minutes, she and the man to whom she had been married for over six years would meet for the last time as husband and wife. The day, cold and blustery in the January wind, was in sharp contrast to the warm summer morning ages ago when she and Greg had climbed these same steps with such vigor and enthusiasm in search of the license which would enable them to legalize forever their commitment to each other. Only moments before, while passing by the church in which they had been married, she had been all too aware that her journey that morning had taken her, in reverse, over the same route which she had followed almost seven years ago, when in all seriousness she and Greg had vowed to love each other so long as they both should live.

The streets—almost deserted except for the work crew dismantling the manger scene and Christmas tree which had adorned the town square for many holiday seasons—reminded her of some public event when all activity had been halted and a moment of silence requested in memory of a famous person who had died. In her darkest moments after they had decided on divorce, she had sometimes found herself thinking of the divorce hearing as the final rites for a dead relationship, her feelings similar to those experienced when she had attended funerals for close relatives or friends.

Forcing herself to open the door to the judge's waiting room, she was surprised to see that her husband had already arrived.

He appeared to be engrossed in a two-day-old newspaper, and he lifted his eyes only long enough to mutter "good morning" before returning his attention to an account of recent NFL playoff action. Before Jan could sit down, the combination secretary and receptionist paused in her phone conversation long enough to inform her that her attorney was already with the judge and that she and her husband could go on back to his office.

With a politeness not displayed in long months of bickering and name-calling, Greg opened the door for his wife to enter the room where the judge, grandfatherly in appearance, stooped and somewhat slovenly, sat behind a desk piled high with books, correspondence, and legal documents. Alert and sensitive to the feelings and needs of the couple now before him, his comments were in keeping with Jan's image of him as a grandfather or favorite uncle involved in a situation in which some beloved member of his family was enduring great personal pain or suffering.

By comparison the young attorney, impeccably but conservatively dressed, seemed bored by the proceedings and appeared anxious to get the whole thing over with as soon as possible. Although she knew that he had handled the case in a very professional manner and that her interests had been well taken care of, Jan could not help feeling that he would be the only one who would in any real way profit from her divorce. As if unaware of her presence or the hurt she was feeling, he read in a flat and monotonous voice the conditions agreed on by both parties in the divorce.

No longer interested in the document itself, Jan could see from the corner of her eye that Greg was blankly staring straight ahead. Having convinced herself that she had no more tears to shed, she was afraid that she was about to cry again. Looking now more directly at her husband, she thought that she could detect a slight trembling of his lips also, although he continued to look at the attorney as if interested only in what he had to say.

Lost in her own thoughts, Jan was unaware that the lawyer had stopped reading. Jerked abruptly back to the present, she recovered in time to hear the judge announce that the divorce would be granted. Remaining only long enough for her attorney to give her some official-looking paper, Jan left without speaking to Greg.

Entering the ladies' room, where she planned to remain until Greg had had enough time to leave, Jan ran a comb absently through her hair, which she had not thought to brush before entering the building. Telling herself that it no longer made any difference anyway, she was nonetheless surprised that she had appeared in court in what was to her such a state of disarray. As if aware of her image for the first time, Jan stared back at herself from the mirror that ran the entire length of the ladies' room and saw that she appeared gaunt and unattractive and, in her opinion, much older than a woman her age had any right to look. Although she was still only twenty-seven years old, the last eight months had seemed like an eternity, an eternity in which she had watched her marriage fall apart bit by bit, day by day, until there was nothing left but bitterness and disillusionment.

Still stunned by the suddenness and ease with which seven years had been wiped out as if they had never existed and afraid that Greg might not yet be gone, Jan moved slowly down the corridor to an exit on the opposite side of the courthouse from which she had entered. Seeing no sign of him, she moved quickly to her car. With the hope that no one had seen her, she edged her compact car cautiously into the traffic, which was now quite heavy with workers from a nearby industrial plant rushing madly to convenient lunch counters and restaurants for their half-hour lunch break.

Although friends had attempted to bolster her spirits by joking of her freedom and the fun she could have as a single woman again, Jan felt as defeated and useless as the discarded Christmas tree now being loaded on the back of the city garbage truck. Bewildered and overwhelmed by a deep sense of failure, she tried to tell herself that she was still young and that things would get better. Though she knew deep inside that this was true, she could only envision more sleepless nights and days of frustration and depression in the weeks ahead.

Still unable to believe that this had happened to her, she

managed to jockey her car onto the recently opened freeway which would enable her to be at home shortly with the four-year-old son she had left crying over his father's absence just an hour earlier.

****

The most common myth about marriage is that two people marry and live happily ever after. Equally disturbing are the new myths about divorce which have encouraged some people to change partners as easily as they change clothes. Many now view divorce as the doorway to a new world of enchantment and excitement, a release from a relationship they have come to see as restrictive and unproductive.

Unfortunately, those who see divorce as a passport to a new life of happiness are frequently just as disappointed as those who have a view of marriage as a cure-all or as one long and uninterrupted state of bliss.

While the breakdown of marriages and families is the most serious social problem facing our world today, it should come as no surprise when one considers the many difficulties and problems which must be encountered and resolved along the way.

Indeed, experts in human relations tell us that a successful marriage is the most challenging task which human beings undertake and yet it is one of the few tasks which requires no proof whatever of competency or awareness of what lies ahead. When one considers the cavalier attitude toward the selection of a marriage partner and the lack of preparation for matrimony, it is surprising that the failure rate is not higher. Even those who have already suffered one marital disaster often go out and choose partners with characteristics similar to those of their former spouses, or they choose mates who are altogether different, which can be just as bad.

While a good marriage is one of life's greatest rewards, the divorce scene depicted above is being re-enacted again and again in ever increasing numbers in courthouses and judges' chambers throughout this country. So commonplace has divorce become that we are told that two out of every five marriages now end in divorce, and some predict that the number will soon reach fifty percent. In certain areas of the country, this percentage has already been exceeded.

We would not be so naive as to imply that there are any simple answers to such a far-reaching and complex problem. Neither do we believe that we have some special gift which entitles us to speak with unquestioned authority on the prerequisites for a good marriage.

We do believe, however, that an awareness of some of the kinds of conflicts and problems which most often lead to divorce can help couples in their struggle to avoid divorce or a marriage which results in unhappiness and tragedy. In the following chapter we will come face to face with some of these unhappy couples as they relate to you in their own words the series of events which have led to the breakdowns of their marriages.

CHAPTER 2.

couples speak

Can we make it together? Will our marriage last? Are we suited for each other? Will our relationship be a happy one? How can we know if we are about to make a bad choice? Will we be compatible as husband and wife?

Couples usually raise these or similar questions and doubts at some time before becoming engaged or married. While we do not profess to know all the answers to such questions, we do know some of the things which go into the making of a troubled marriage. We have learned from our experience in working with married couples that certain problems keep cropping up too often to be ignored as major factors in producing marriages which end in divorce.

This is not to imply that there are marriages which never encounter problems. Quite the contrary. All marriages have problems because human beings are involved, and all human beings have emotional hang-ups and undesirable personality traits or characteristics in varying degrees. All human beings have doubts about themselves and occasionally experience difficulty in relating to others. However, most learn to live with themselves and others relatively well.

There are, however, some individuals in whom problems of personal and social adjustment seem more severe than in others. In many cases these same people bring to a marriage certain personality characteristics, unresolved conflicts, personal problems, or ways of thinking and behaving which make living with them intolerable.

Despite the fact that marrying such a person greatly increases the chances for a difficult marriage, it is amazing how often clues to possible future trouble are ignored. While many claim that their spouses developed or acquired these undesirable traits or behaviors after marriage, it is our contention that this just isn't so in most cases. It is our belief that many of the problems which led to conflict or divorce were present before marriage. At least the potential or seeds for dissension were already there. Unfortunately, they were ignored or played down, only to surface after marriage, with disastrous results for all.

It is worth noting that most people are vitally concerned with the social, physical, moral, intellectual, and economic qualifications of their soon-to-be wife or husband. Unfortunately, the same careful attention is not always given to matters such as emotional stability, personality dynamics, personal attitudes, and ways of thinking and behaving, even though these things have more to do with success or failure in marriage than other factors with which we are more concerned.

While it must be admitted that the assessment of personality or the measurement of attitudes or ways of thinking and behaving is much more difficult than the evaluation of social status, the size of a bank account, family background, or level of education, cues or signals are in most cases available and can be of considerable value to those seriously interested in learning more about the person they are about to marry.

If certain problems do indeed tend to crop up again and again in marriages that end in divorce, how does one avoid involvement in such a relationship? What are these problems, and how are they manifested? How does one recognize a man or woman who is likely to be a poor marriage risk? What signs might indicate that marriage to one specific human being would be a mistake?

In our attempt to answer some of the questions raised above, we decided that the best approach would be to let couples speak for themselves, with our role being primarily that of recorder. With this kind of sharing, our readers can see for themselves first-hand the kinds of problems which cause the most conflict in marriage. Many of the individuals presented eventually divorced.

Those already married can learn to recognize some early warning signals that, if heeded, could prevent marriage problems from developing into full-blown crises. Unmarried readers will have the opportunity to see some of the dangers and pitfalls which may lie ahead if these signals are ignored during the dating period.

The presence of these or similar problems in any couple's relationship should raise a red flag. It is our hope that the individuals involved will stop and ask: Do I really want to marry this person? What does this behavior mean? What will it be like if this behavior continues after marriage?

Assuming that most people want to avoid making a mistake in the selection of a husband or wife, the purpose of this chapter is to share some of the mistakes which others have made in choosing a marriage partner. Based on experiences shared with us by couples whose marriages have broken down, suggestions for maximizing your chances of choosing an unsuitable marriage partner are offered.

marry someone with vastly different views of the roles of men and women in marriage

Freda and Theo had two children, ages thirteen and eleven, and had been married for fifteen years when they scheduled their first appointment with a marriage and family counselor. Insisting that they had always gotten along well with each other until recently, both agreed that they were having trouble communicating with their children. Their son, age thirteen, had been arrested several months earlier and placed on probation after he and one of his friends had confessed to breaking windows in a local high school. Their eleven-year-old daughter had become very belligerent and increasingly difficult to manage. While Freda and Theo viewed a certain amount of disagreement and rebelliousness as normal, they agreed that they felt they were losing control of their children and no longer knew how to cope with the situation. Any attempt to get them to help with the chores around the house met with great resistance and usually ended with the father having to threaten to discipline them in some way. Again both parents agreed that this was a departure from earlier times, when the children had usually managed to complete their assignments reasonably well. Though their children were previously very good students, their son had made two failing grades the past quarter, while their daughter had dropped one letter grade in most of her subjects.

At this point in the conversation Theo interrupted his wife to ask in obvious anger, "Why don't you go ahead and tell him the real reason they have changed?" Peeved by her husband's outburst, Freda replied, "Why don't you tell him yourself, since you think you know all the answers?"

Seeming to be both hurt and angry, Theo responded by saying that they had had ideal marriage and family relationships until Freda had decided that being a wife and mother was not enough for her. Theo then expressed in no uncertain terms his feeling that the problems with the children had begun as a result of Freda's not being where she belonged—at home with the children.

In subsequent sessions it was revealed that Freda had first expressed a desire to apply for a teaching job when her younger child had entered the first grade. Although she had a degree in education, she had not taught since she had married Theo when she graduated from college. While Theo had opposed the idea from the beginning, he had succumbed to his wife's desires after a family discussion in which all had participated. All had agreed that they could use the extra money and that they would be willing to chip in and help around the house so that Freda could teach in a nearby school. Things had gone well until Freda discovered that she would have to go back to school on weekends and during the summer in order to renew her teaching certificate. The children had cooperated for a while but had rebelled more and more as the duties around the house increased. Both husband and children protested more vociferously as Freda's time away from home increased because of the demands of her job and schooling. As a consequence, meals were prepared in a haphazard fashion, and the house became, in Theo's words, "a disaster area."

Attacking his wife further, Theo said that he could not understand Freda's sudden desire to pursue a career. Indicating that they had discussed the issue many times prior to marriage, he reminded Freda of her expressed lack of interest in anything other than being a good wife and mother. Insisting that he had given her everything that she had ever asked for, he could not understand her unhappiness. They lived in one of the nicer sections of town, she had her own sports car, was a member of the country club, and had a host of friends. He concluded by saying that he had tried in every way he knew to adjust to Freda's working outside the home, but that he could no longer take it, and that something had to be done.

When her husband sat back in his chair, Freda admitted that her husband had been correct in regard to her stated commitment, prior to marriage, to her husband and children. "And at the time," Freda said, "I honestly felt that I could be happy just being a good wife and mother. I really had no interest or motivation to go out into the world and find a job of any kind. The idea of staying at home and keeping house for the man I loved and taking care of our children really appealed to me when I was twenty-two. After several years, however, I discovered that keeping house and taking care of children was not enough. I became bored and dissatisfied. My unhappiness began to show in the way I related to my children and my husband. I was short and ill-tempered with everybody. Once I became involved in meaningful work outside the home, I gradually began to feel better about myself and as a result found myself able to respond to my husband and children with far more love and affection than before."

Turning to her husband, Freda said that the problems had begun when Theo had had to cancel some of his plans in order to stay with the children on weekends and evenings when she had to be in school or at the university. When they had tried to work out a schedule which would be satisfying to both, they had been unsuccessful.

Although she insisted that she loved her family dearly, Freda concluded that she had no intention of giving up her work, since she felt that she had a right to a life which included more than just being a housewife. Admitting that his wife had been very successful and effective as a teacher, Theo countered with the argument that she had paid a big price for her success; gross neglect of her children and husband. Disagreeing vehemently, Freda insisted that, on the contrary, she had become a better mother and companion.

Discussion

While we would agree that it is a matter of utmost importance, our purpose is not to become embroiled in the controversy of the woman's role in marriage. Our purpose is instead that of calling attention to the large number of marriages which run into serious problems as a consequence of husbands' and wives' different attitudes on this crucial issue.

Until fairly recent times, whenever divorce became an issue, it seemed that it was usually the male who instigated such thinking. More recently, however, it seems that more and more women are taking the initiative in asking for a separation or divorce. While many do not go to this extreme, they are certainly more vocal and demanding in their desire for more freedom and independence to pursue a life-style which can be meaningful for them. The number of women willing to settle for a career as housewife and mother seems to be decreasing each year. More and more women are saying that marriage is just not enough; many say they want more out of life than merely being a good wife and mother. If the number of couples coming to marriage counselors with this as a major area of conflict can be used as an indicator, then it can be said that the problem is one of major proportions in all segments of our society.

Whether or not Freda's going to work is a major factor in the problems existing with the children is open to debate. Undoubtedly there are many marriages and families which are disrupted by such a turn of events. The role of working wives and mothers has been cussed and discussed for years. Just as some will insist that homes have been destroyed when women insist on pursuing outside interests or careers, others will argue that their family situations have improved when the wife or mother is happily and successfully working outside the home.

There are many changes which have made it possible for women to discover for themselves careers and pursuits which add to their lives a meaningful dimension which they have not found in being "just a housewife." Some of these changes are: the increase in day-care centers for small children, the opening up of more career opportunities for women as a result of anti-discriminatory laws, the women's liberation movement, the increase in divorce, greater assertiveness on the part of women, and, probably the most important of all, the recognition of and insistence by women themselves that they are just as capable of entering the mainstream of life as their male counterparts. Other women, especially those who have never worked or supported themselves before marriage, often say, "I just want to prove I can make it on my own." For reasons such as these, many counselors recommend that individuals work for at least a year before they marry. While many women still feel that being a wife and mother is the highest calling in the world, others feel that they have other significant contributions to make.

Whatever the causes, the trend of women pursuing careers outside marriage is apt to continue. While each couple will have to decide what is right for them, we cannot emphasize too strongly how important it is that couples have some sense of agreement before marriage regarding their roles after marriage, unless they are prepared to live with considerable conflict in the years ahead. Even when couples go to great lengths to assure each other that they are in harmony concerning what they expect after marriage, problems can arise at a later date. As with Freda, wives can change even when their feelings are pretty definite prior to marriage. Also, even though many husbands encourage their wives to feel free and independent, they often have great difficulty making the adjustment if their wives later decide to pursue a career.

While much publicity has been centered around the housewife who wants to work outside the home after marriage, there are many cases in which controversy has arisen when the couple enters marriage with the understanding that the wife will actively pursue a career of her own and contribute to the support of the family. On these occasions conflict has developed when the wife decides she no longer wants to work. For example, one couple on the verge of divorce came for counseling with the complaint that the wife had decided that she no longer wanted to work but wanted to stay at home and devote her full time to raising a family. Because of the reduction in income, the husband complained that many adjustments in their way of living had resulted. Their two children were also complaining that they now felt smothered and over-protected by a mother who had decided that she needed to spend most of her time seeing that her children were well taken care of. Often such women say, "My family is my whole life."

It is important for couples entering marriage in their early twenties to be aware of the possibility of personality growth and change which normally takes place in every individual. Aspirations and goals can and will change in the course of moving from one life stage to another. It is unrealistic for a husband or wife to expect that a spouse's commitment to being a housewife, for example, will continue indefinitely and with the same vigor with which it was made at age twenty-one. Couples need change, individuals need change, and children need change. What a couple could more realistically commit themselves to when contemplating marriage is trying to be responsive to one another's needs as both grow and change together. This attitude can help a couple avoid the kind of dead-end street Freda and Theo have reached. A wife who wants to return to work could add variety and excitement to a marriage and to family life if the couple looked upon this change as a challenge rather than as a threat to the stability of their relationship.

marry to escape a
bad family situation

Maria and Wiley had been married for two years when Maria came alone to talk with the marriage counselor. Although she insisted that she still loved her husband, she was finding it more and more difficult to make a go of it as a result of his reluctance to work and the subsequent accumulation of unpaid bills. Whenever bill collectors came to the apartment demanding payment, Wiley handled the situation by not answering the door. If he suspected a phone call might be from a bill collector, he wouldn't answer it.

When Maria asked him to look for a job, Wiley usually responded that the jobs offered him were demeaning and that he would not be panicked into taking work which he did not find challenging.

At first reluctant to criticize or speak in negative terms about Wiley, Maria admitted to the counselor in the second session that she had just about concluded that Wiley was not very ambitious and preferred lying around the house all day getting stoned or looking at sex magazines to putting in an honest day's work.

Despite this admission, however, in discussing her plans for the future Maria continued to express the hope that she and Wiley could still get it together. Working full time as a secretary, she was also going to college full time at night and hoped to graduate in three years, at age twenty-one, with a degree in business. As a freshman she had maintained an A average. Wiley, on the other hand, at age twenty-three, had flunked out of several colleges. Having gone to college off and on for three years, both prior to and since their marriage, he was still classified as a freshman.

In response to the counselor's question regarding the obvious differences in goals and levels of achievement, Maria said that Wiley was a very intelligent person and that she still hoped that he would eventually find himself and work with her toward a goal which would be rewarding for both of them.

In discussing her reasons for marrying Wiley, Maria said that she would have done anything to get away from her parents and her home situation. Although her parents had remained married, they had talked of divorce as long as Maria could remember. She could still recall the many nights she and her brother had cried themselves to sleep after listening to their parents' heated arguments and threats to leave each other. Describing her mother as an intellectual snob who never ceased to remind her children that their father was a miserable failure, Maria said that her mother had told her on numerous occasions that she had remained married to her husband only because of the children.

When she discussed her mother further, Maria revealed that she had never shown any affection to either her husband or her children but had berated them almost constantly about their lack of ambition and desire to make something of themselves. A woman who would fly into a rage for no apparent reason, she would suddenly change and a few minutes later act as if nothing had happened. Although she never abused them physically and saw to it that her children were well clothed and fed, Maria said that her mother had made life miserable for both her children and her husband with her never-ending complaining and fussing. Things were so bad at times that "I used to hope that she would give me up for adoption," Maria reported.

When asked to talk about her relationship with her father, Maria said, "We never had one." He spent long hours at his service station and managed his business well. When he came home, however, he almost never spoke to his children and only to his wife after she continued to harangue him until he was provoked into saying something which usually started a violent argument. He chose to spend most of his time watching television or secluded with his paper in the bedroom upstairs where he slept alone. When asked if he ever spanked or physically abused his children, Maria responded that "he never paid us that much attention. On those rare occasions when he would scold us for interrupting his television show or for getting too many phone calls, it would be a welcome change from the rest of the time, when he seemed totally unaware of our existence."

In discussing her parents further, Maria said that about the only thing they ever agreed on was that she could not date until after graduation from high school. Maria indicated that this had made no difference, since boys never asked her out in high school anyway.

According to Maria, however, this changed rather suddenly when she met Wiley as a freshman in a community college they both attended in a nearby city. For the first time in her life, Maria reported, someone seemed interested in her and asked her out. While Maria was still not permitted to go out at night, they managed to find time between classes to see each other. Wiley appeared to be interested in her and was lavish in his attention and praise. Maria said that she came to see in him the opportunity to establish with another human being a relationship in which she could get the love and attention she had never before received.

When he asked her in the second week of their relationship to have sex with him, she had not hesitated. Although she had not found the sex pleasurable, she said that the closeness and affection proved to be most satisfying.

Somewhat surprised when Wiley had begun to ask her for money (which he never repaid) to pay for their lunch or to buy his books, Maria said that she would have given him the moon if he had asked for it in return for what he had given her. When she had gone a step further and expressed a willingness to take a full-time job to support them while Wiley went to school during the day, he had proposed. Although her mother had fought the marriage, Maria and Wiley had run away and married. (Maria again informed the counselor that she would have done anything to get away from her home and parents.) The only thing which had prevented her from running away from home years earlier had been the responsibility she had felt for her younger brother, she said. Rather than opposing the marriage, her father had, in her opinion, been glad to get rid of her.

Discussion

Unfortunately for Maria, she married Wiley with unrealistic expectations of what marriage could do for her. She expected him to save her from a home that had been unhappy all her life, to provide the love and attention that she had never received, and to fulfill her needs for friendship and satisfying relationships with others.

Sometimes it is impossible for an individual who has been emotionally abused as a child *not* to respond to someone who offers affection and love, even if the price for closeness is additional rejection and abuse. Maria's hunger for love was so enormous that when she married Wiley it was probably not possible for her to consider the fact that he was already using her for financial support and would more than likely do so in the future.

It is too often easy to see in a prospective marriage partner the "answer" to long-term emotional needs and to overlook in the future spouse behaviors which indeed may defeat the very needs which are looking for fulfillment.

Marriages under such conditions are almost inevitably doomed from the beginning because of the unrealistic expectations of one or both partners. Despite the poor prognosis for those who enter marriage under these circumstances, the number who marry to escape an unhappy home life seems to be quite sizable.

marry while still a teenager

Vera informed the marriage counselor that she could no longer stand the thought of her husband, Chan, touching her. Whenever she attempted to have sex, it was so painful she could hardly endure it. Penetration had been impossible in recent attempts, and Vera insisted that she was so tense that she could feel her pelvic muscles tighten up. Even when Chan wanted to kiss her, she found it so repulsive that she wanted to throw up. She had grown so grouchy that they argued most of the time. She said, "It seems as if I go out of my way to find something to criticize Chan for. He can never please me, and I am so picky I don't even like myself. Even the most insignificant things about him irritate me."

In response to the counselor's probing, Vera said that she had married Chan when she was a senior in high school. Chan had graduated the previous year. Now twenty-five, Vera said with considerable feeling that she had never had a chance to be independent or to prove to herself and others that she could make it on her own. Her parents had been very protective and authoritarian and had assumed most of the responsibility for their daughter's life. Marriage to Chan had, in Vera's opinion, only resulted in a transfer of her dependence from her parents to Chan. "In general, he ran my life and made most of the decisions in our marriage."

In the second session Vera revealed that neither she nor Chan had ever dated anyone else. They had dated since the tenth grade, and Vera said that she had recently begun to resent the fact that she had not had a chance to date other guys while in high school. Although Chan insisted that he wanted to stay married, Vera said that she had noticed him around other women in recent months and had become convinced that he too resented the lack of past opportunities to date others. Admitting that she could understand rationally why he would flirt with other women, she confessed that it still made her jealous when he did. His insistence that he had never been unfaithful to her did little to allay her fear that he would someday leave her for another woman as a result of his curiosity and desire to be involved with more than one woman in his lifetime. Vera continued, "And I can understand his need because I find myself wondering what it would be like to know other men. I feel awfully guilty when I do, but recently it has become almost an obsession with me. I really find myself excited when other men express interest in me. Although I could never mess around with another man while I am married to Chan, I feel shortchanged in that I committed myself so early to just one man. It really bugs me that I will never know what it is like to have an intimate or deep relationship with anyone else."

Obviously hurt and confused, Vera began to discuss the deep and intense feelings she and Chan had once had for each other. "We were so very much in love, but something happened. We had so much fun that we wanted to spend every minute together. We agreed that ours would be a marriage made in heaven and would surely last forever. We never seemed to get tired of each other and eventually decided to marry so we would not have to be apart. We were so turned on by each other that we would sit for hours kissing and hugging. Although we did not go all the way until just before marriage, we did everything else, and I would never have thought that someday I would be turned off by his caresses. We can't even talk anymore. When I try to discuss our relationship with Chan, he just clams up or goes into another room."

Discussion

Teenagers usually resent their parents' referring to their relationships with other boys and girls as "puppy love" or "infatuation." To be told that they are just going through a stage and that their feelings for that special person will someday wane is equally unacceptable.

While older people can make such comments with reasonable confidence that they are correct because of their personal experiences, young people have no reservoir of experience from which to reach such a conclusion. During adolescence they are the victims of some of the most intense feelings they will ever have. Their feelings are *now*. They have no desire or inclination to be patient or to postpone gratification. Why look for something better or spend long hours analyzing and exploring a relationship when each moment with that special someone is pure ecstasy? Never mind that their concept of love and marriage is straight out of Hollywood or that their range of sexual and romantic encounters has been colored to a large degree by what they have been exposed to in books, magazines, and television.

While such romantic fantasies can provide pleasant interludes from the more mundane and realistic world in which human beings live out their existence, it is important that the concept of love and marriage held by most teenagers not be internalized to the point that they rid themselves of any reasonable chance to build a good marriage based on more realistic views of life with another person.

Unfortunately, most teenagers do enter marriage with many unrealistic and artificial expectations regarding love, sex, marriage, and family. While playing house or living in a make-believe world of rose-covered cottages and sexual wonderlands can be a most pleasant pastime for teenagers, they need to be confronted with the harsh reality that life is seldom what it is painted to be in Hollywood and on television. Despite all their dreams of "living happily ever after," we are confronted with the cold hard statistics which suggest that the prognosis for teenagers to marry is a rather dismal one. While the odds against the survival of marriage at any age are increasing, those for teenage marriages are much worse.

When a person makes a decision to marry at a young age, he or she makes one of life's most important decisions on the basis of an extremely meager pool of information and experience. No matter how hard teenagers try to convince themselves otherwise, there is no substitute for experience in interpersonal relationships. While people continue to change and grow as long as they live, more mature couples have at least made some progress and achieved some stability in regard to their values and goals in life. Most have been involved in a number of relationships with other human beings and have an accumulation of knowledge and experience on which a more intelligent decision can be made.

The problems encountered in early marriages are too numerous to be detailed here. Suffice it to say that those experienced by Vera and Chan are quite typical. They may include such feelings and difficulties as disillusionment, resentment, jealousy, sexual conflicts, problems with communication, going in separate directions in regard to goals, interests, and values as they grow older, financial woes, educational and career differences, and the hardship of trying to be parents while still in many ways children themselves.

While all of these problems are encountered frequently in counseling with couples who married prematurely, none is heard with such frequency as that of a "sense of loss" or "being deprived of something of great importance." While stated in various forms, such a complaint usually goes something like this: "I feel as if I have been cheated out of something," or "I feel as if I have missed out on the opportunity to be with other people my age and to prove that I could make it on my own."

Although sex seems to be the source of many of their difficulties, it soon becomes apparent that the sexual conflicts between Vera and Chan are only the obvious symptoms of more basic problems in their marriage. Convinced that their love would endure forever, both Vera and Chan are disenchanted and puzzled when their marriage begins to crumble after only a few years.

While the break-up of a marriage is difficult at any age, it seems particularly devastating for teenagers who have gone into it with such idealistic and romantic expectations. Not only are they ill-prepared to handle marriage; they usually are not prepared to handle the erosion of the relationship and the shattered hopes and dreams which inevitably result for those who enter marriage with such unrealistic expectations.

Faced with a situation similar to the one described by Vera, and plagued with feelings of guilt and the belief that marriage should be forever, some couples insist on staying together despite many problems. Others find the frustrations too many and the temptations too great and call it quits. Some manage to hold the marriage together for fifteen or twenty years before they decide they are not going to spend the rest of their lives being deprived of some of the things they missed out on because they married at such an early age. These are often the middle-aged men and women seen running frantically from place to place and partner to partner in search of their lost youth or in search of some meaningful relationship before it is too late.

While we have focused in this case on youthful marriages, it should also be emphasized that older people can and do make the same mistake. It is, for example, not uncommon to see a thirty-year-old woman who has never dated or been very successful in male-female relationships accept the first person who pays her any serious attention. Or a thirty-five-year-old man who has been deprived of female companionship (for a variety of reasons) may settle, out of desperation, for anyone who comes along. Many such men and women say, "I am desperate," "This is my last chance," "I'm already thirty and I don't want to end up an old maid," or "I don't want to spend the rest of my life as a lonely old man." While different from Vera and Chan in age, such couples may still be children when it comes to experience in intimate and meaningful relationships.

In summary, it should be said that the choice of a husband or wife should be based on the most reliable sources of information and knowledge available, both quantitatively and qualitatively. This pool of knowledge can be acquired only with a variety of experiences and contacts with other males and females over an extended period of time. Unfortunately, time and experience are the things teenagers most often lack.

marry someone who cannot tolerate closeness or intimacy

"I feel like my husband doesn't want to be alone with me or spend time with me," thirty-five-year-old June complained to the counselor. "Richard says he loves me, and I want to believe it, but when there is an opportunity for us to be just with each other, it seems something always interferes, and he doesn't do anything to avoid intrusions. Last weekend we made plans to be at home alone, but Saturday morning at 9:30 he said he needed to check the air conditioner at the trailer we rent out and he'd be back in an hour. He didn't get home until 12:30 p.m., and he brought his two children to spend the rest of the weekend with us. He said the weather was so nice that it would be a shame to waste it staying at home. He decided that the four of us would go to the lake for a picnic on Sunday. He didn't have to bring the children; it wasn't their weekend to visit. When I reminded him that we had planned to spend the weekend alone he said, 'We spend every night of the week with each other.' To me that's different, but he doesn't think so. Last summer when he had a month's vacation, he spent every day playing golf at the country club. He said he didn't want to go on a trip because it was too hot and crowded on the highways, but he played golf on a crowded course in the July sun for five hours every day. He has to go to a lot of out-of-town meetings in his work. I have asked him many times to take me along, but he refuses. He says I'd be bored. Richard is a good husband in many ways and a good provider, but I feel lonely living with him. I would like for us to be friends and companions, but he doesn't seem to want to. I even went back to work to have something to fill my time."

After listening patiently to his wife, Richard turned to the counselor: "June nags me about being alone with her. I can't just sit at home all the time. It makes me nervous. I like to be on the go, and I like to have plans for a weekend. It bores me to death to lie around the house when there's nothing to do there. I like June. She's attractive, a good cook and housekeeper, and a good entertainer when we have company. I'm always proud to take her places with me, but I don't know how we'd get along if we spent too much time together. I don't know what we would do together or what we would talk about. If we spent four or five days alone, we might find out we have nothing in common. June might get bored with me. I don't know."

Discussion

Some people are afraid to be emotionally close to anyone, including their spouses. This need to keep some distance between themselves and others can arise for a variety of reasons, but the results can create enormous frustration in a marriage. June's desire to have time alone with her husband in order to develop friendship and companionship in their marriage is appropriate. Richard's fear of being unable to be companionable with his wife is obvious. June's reluctance to intrude upon this fear and Richard's efforts to keep some distance have created barriers which have aroused feelings of rejection and resentment between them.

If there is reason to suspect that differences in the need for closeness and intimacy exist between individuals in a relationship, the following questions should be raised.

(1) What are the results when plans to do something together include no one but the couple?

(2) How do we feel when we are alone with each other?

(3) Does either partner consistently make plans which keep us apart?

(4) Do we share experiences?

(5) Can we talk for long periods of time with ease?

(6) Does either partner seem uncomfortable in intimate situations?

(7) Can we relax in each other's presence without being involved in some activity?

(8) Are our needs for closeness reasonably similar?

We do not want to give the impression that individuals who prefer distance in a relationship are necessarily doomed to have a poor marriage. As long as the two people involved are reasonably compatible in their needs for distance or closeness, they may get along well together. The problem arises when one has a strong need for intimacy and closeness, while the other feels smothered after marriage.

marry someone who is unwilling to accept change in the other

After eleven years of marriage to Reeves, Lola reported that she had awakened at three the previous night and suddenly come to the conclusion that she did not love her husband anymore. Although she had been aware that the excitement and zest which she had felt in the first few years of marriage had slowly disappeared, she said that she had been unable to put her finger on any certain cause for the decline in her feelings for her husband.

Unable to go back to sleep, she had awakened her husband when she had gone to the kitchen for a glass of milk. When she failed to return to bed, he had come looking for her. For the first time in years, Lola said, they sat in the kitchen and had a serious discussion about their relationship with each other. They had both felt overwhelmed with sadness as a result of having lost something which had at one time been beautiful, and both admitted that somewhere along the line they had begun to grow apart, gradually going their separate ways. The gap had widened in recent years to the point that they had even ceased to argue about issues which had earlier caused considerable dissension between them.

When questioned about these issues, Lola said that when she married Reeves he had been employed as a shipping clerk in a large department store, having dropped out of college in his second year. They had met in her father's clothing store, where she worked as a salesperson. After dating for ten months, they had decided to marry, and Reeves had agreed to come to work for her father with the idea that he would one day take over the business.

Lola said that things had gone along smoothly for the first year. In the second year, however, Reeves had become involved in several heated arguments with his father-in-law, who said that

Reeves was not doing his share of the work. When Lola began crying after he threatened to quit, Reeves promised that he would give it another six months. Things continued to worsen, however, and in September Reeves informed Lola that he had decided to go back to college and prepare himself to teach. When Lola shouted that she had no intention of giving up the standard of living to which she was accustomed to live instead on a school teacher's salary, Reeves responded that he had already enrolled in school for the fall quarter. Though Lola's parents opposed her leaving, Lola had, after long hours of fighting, agreed to take a small apartment near the university and get a job to help pay expenses.

With considerable help from Lola's father, Reeves had graduated in two years. Much to Lola's dismay, however, Reeves told her that he had been accepted in graduate school and hoped to do well enough to go ahead and eventually get his doctorate in history.

Although she resisted, Lola had again given in and agreed to stay with Reeves. For the next four years Lola continued to work at her job as a secretary, being promoted to the position of office manager in her third year. When Reeves accused her of being more interested in her work than in helping him get through graduate school, Lola admitted that she had initially detested the thought of having to work after marriage but had gradually grown to find the work challenging and interesting.

After a number of confrontations about her long hours, Lola retaliated by charging that Reeves was never at home anyway but always at the library or engaged in rap sessions with his fellow students after class hours. Interpreting Reeves' involvement with his studies as an indication that he no longer cared for her, Lola told the counselor that when they had married Reeves had shown no interest in continuing his education and had promised instead to work toward a career in business, which they both saw as being far more lucrative than teaching. Her disappointment had become even greater when she learned that he expected her to support him while he went to college. Each time she had thought the end was in sight, he had decided to prolong his studies. The more he became involved in school, the less she saw of him at home. It was at this point that Lola said she had thrown herself into her work with vigor, determined to make a life for herself.

After graduation Reeves accepted a job teaching at a university in another state. Lola took a job as an executive secretary in a big company with a salary nearly as large as Reeves'. It was about this time, according to Lola, that all efforts at communicating stopped. Reeves accused Lola of being interested in business and nothing else. Lola countered that she found it boring to listen to Reeves talk about nothing but his research and teaching at the university.

Although they had initially planned to have children, Lola balked at the idea as the years passed, accusing Reeves of wanting children in order to keep her at home. Admitting that he had married Lola with the idea that she was primarily interested in being a wife and mother, Reeves said that he had never been able to accept her refusal to follow through with their agreement to have a family—something which they had discussed at great length prior to marriage. Although Reeves still felt that he had been deceived, Lola said that he had given up trying to convince her to have children and had instead thrown himself even more into his work.

When Lola informed her husband of her sessions with a marriage counselor, Reeves replied that it was a good time to discuss something he had been wanting to bring up for a long time. He proceeded to tell Lola that he had fallen in love with a graduate student at the university and wanted a divorce.

Although Lola insisted that she had not been surprised when Reeves told her this, she confessed that she had been hurt. Lola agreed to the divorce and informed the counselor that while the break-up of the marriage saddened her, they had in essence been divorced for several years. Confessing that she had spent long hours trying to figure out what had happened to the love they once had for each other, Lola said that she had come to the conclusion that they had both changed so much that they did not even faintly resemble the people they had been eleven years ago.

While both had been successful in their careers, Lola said, "We went in different directions and neither was able or willing to accept the changes in the other person. As the years passed, we grew so far apart that there was nothing left on which we could build a marriage."

Discussion

Married couples grow apart for many reasons. However, one of the major reasons given for this occurrence is that of change. A woman recently said, "My husband is not the same man I married. He has changed so much that I feel as if I am married to a total stranger." The husband replied that he had not really changed that much but that his wife surely had. "In the first years of our marriage she was kind and considerate and seemed interesting in building a home for me and the children. In the last few years, however, she has rebelled against everything she once stood for and seems intent on a career apart from that of wife and mother."

While they were never able to agree on who had done the changing, they were able to agree that it had occurred and that their marriage was sheer chaos as a result.

The truth is that both had changed after eight years of marriage, and neither was able to adjust to the change in the other.

If we assume that most couples marry because they love each other, then we can conclude that all marriages ending in divorce do so because of changes in the feelings of the two people involved.

Although it may seem trite to repeat that which is so obvious, we do so because many couples embark on a life together with the unspoken assumption that things will always be the same and that both parties will forever remain as they were when they were dating. It should be stressed, however, that marriage is a process, a process in which change is inevitable. While most of us strive for stability in life, there are few things in this world which are stable or permanent. Things change. People are changing all the time. No person is exactly the same today as he or she was yesterday. Consequently, all relationships are also continuously undergoing change, and all come to an end eventually. Even those marriages which are judged successful will eventually come to an end due to death.

Unfortunately, many marriages die prematurely because too many husbands and wives choose to ignore the inescapable fact that people do change.

People can grow apart even when they truly love and care for each other. For some the resistance to change is so deeply ingrained that acceptance of change, even in someone they dearly love, is almost impossible. However, since it is an indisputable fact of life that people do change, and since this is one of the major reasons listed by couples as the source of problems in marriage, couples would do well to explore in depth their ability to adjust to the many changes which are inevitable in the years after marriage.

Difficulties might be anticipated if:

(1) either person seems locked into a way of thinking or behaving which allows for no difference of opinion or new ideas.

(2) either has communicated to the other what he or she wants in a husband or wife and gives the impression that he or she will not tolerate any deviation from this rigid stance, now or in the future.

(3) one of the individuals demonstrates a desire to grow and improve while the other seems determined to maintain the status quo.

(4) one or both shows a noticeable lack of curiosity or interest in the changes which are occurring around him or her from day to day.

(5) one seems eager to experiment and try new things, while the other refuses to depart from more traditional and established ways.

(6) either gets upset easily or acts as if the whole day is ruined if things do not go according to schedule or if plans are changed. The individual who is unable to adjust to change before marriage is not likely to be able to adjust to change after marriage.

marry someone who wants to fuss or fight all the time

Obviously very angry with each other, Norm and Cecile entered the counselor's office and took seats as far apart as possible. Norm said sullenly that he wanted out of the marriage because of the constant fussing and fighting. Cecile agreed that their marriage seemed to be one continuous argument, but said that she did not want a divorce and wanted to try to work things out. Norm interrupted to say that he was so depressed about their relationship that he felt it would be futile to try any more.

Married six years earlier, after dating for five months, Norm and Cecile confessed that they had fought this way even while dating. Before marriage they could get away from each other when their anger got out of hand, so they had ignored the fact that they never seemed to agree on anything. After marriage, however, they had continued to disagree and fight over even the smallest things. Although they would periodically sit down and agree not to get so upset with each other and to control their tempers, they were never able to maintain the peace for any length of time. Norm insisted that he would leave work each day determined not to lose his temper with Cecile. As soon as he entered the house, however, he said it was as if some big change came over him and the slightest thing would upset him. Cecile countered that she felt that she always had to be on guard lest she say or do something which would set Norm off. Again Norm interrupted to say that it seemed as if Cecile went out of her way to antagonize him. No matter what he said or suggested, Cecile took issue with it. He could never get her to be quiet long enough to listen to his views on any subject.

Admitting that she had a mind of her own and didn't appreciate anyone bossing her around, Cecile accused Norm of never hearing her out either. Both agreed that they had never been able to communicate except when arguing. As unpleasant as their communications were, they both felt that this beat no communication at all.

Since they had three children ranging in age from one to five, both Norm and Cecile expressed a reluctance to break up the marriage. Cecile remarked, however, that the children were being affected by the constant conflict. The five-year-old was already showing signs of excessive nervousness and still wet the bed occasionally. All three had problems going to sleep at night and often seemed unduly irritated with each other as well as with other children in the neighborhood.

Returning to their attacks on each other, Norm said that things would improve if Cecile would just listen to him more and avoid doing things which she knew upset him. Cecile replied that she too had resolved in the past not to let Norm upset her, and said that she felt that she had made an honest effort to keep quiet even when she felt as if she were about to explode. At such times she would contain her feelings until Norm would criticize her, and then out of a need for self-preservation she would defend herself by attacking him. This pattern would continue until Norm would explode in what Cecile described as a childish temper tantrum. During such times there was no reasoning with him. Norm himself confessed that when he became this angry he became irrational.

Despite the counselor's attempts to get Norm and Cecile to refrain from interrupting each other and to make a sincere effort to listen when the other spoke, each continued to take issue with anything the other said, even when they were in essence saying the same thing. When the counselor tried to arrange another appointment, they could not agree on the time, and each accused the other of trying to sabotage the sessions. Whenever it appeared that one might be on the verge of making some concessions or expressing a willingness to work at changing some of the destructive ways in which they related to each other, the other would dredge up things from the long-distant past to prove that the partner could not be trusted to do anything to improve their relationship.

Discussion

Although it might appear to an outsider that the relationship between Cecile and Norm would be intolerable, there are couples who seem to thrive on conflict. Many such couples stay married for years even though they insist they cannot tolerate each other. Most would never admit that they need to fight or to make life miserable for themselves or their partner. And yet it seems that neither Norm nor Cecile can tolerate any sort of peaceful coexistence. If things seem to be going along rather smoothly, one or both will do something to torpedo the state of harmony existing between them at the moment.

Unfortunately, couples like this one not only make life miserable for each other; if there are children, they almost inevitably get caught up in such a destructive family relationship and quite often learn similar ways of relating to others.

Couples like Norm and Cecile are extremely difficult to work with in counseling because of the excessive hostility and anger present. The pattern of angry and destructive ways of relating to each other is often so deeply ingrained and the anger so pervasive and intense that it is impossible to break through the wall of resistance even to get them to listen to suggestions as to how they might improve their relationship. In addition, many such couples do not really want to change, even though they express great dissatisfaction with their marriage.

Problems in marriages like that of Norm and Cecile involve much more than just being incompatible or disagreeing on certain issues. Their ways of relating to each other border on the pathological. They seem to delight in hurting each other as well as inflicting pain on themselves. Though there is no evidence that Norm and Cecile actually inflict physical punishment on each other, the mental anguish and unhappiness are undeniable. While we have no desire to go into any discussion of sadistic and masochistic relationships, most laypeople are familiar enough with the terms to suspect that marriages such as the one described above might well fall into this category.

It would be obvious to most individuals that something is wrong if one's intended spouse seems to enjoy inflicting physical punishment on others. This can sometime include such seemingly harmless activities as playing practical jokes which cause excessive embarrassment or discomfort to the victims. While most individuals occasionally engage in such activities, the person who seems to taunt or humiliate others frequently and to enjoy the victims' discomfort should be viewed with caution. Or the person who is always putting others down may fall into this category. Such individuals may, for example, go out of their way to belittle or to make their date look foolish at a social gathering or flirt with other men or women and ignore their spouse or date for the evening.

Certainly marriage to a person who is always fussing or looking for things to fight about would be considered undesirable for most. While it is just as important for couples to learn how to fight as it is for them to learn to love, it should be obvious that marriage to individuals possessing the need for conflict to the degree evidenced by Norm and Cecile would constitute a constant state of siege.

marry someone who is still
clinging to mom and dad

Brett and Cher had been married for four years when Brett made his first appointment with the social worker in the community mental health center where they lived. Although he had begged Cher to accompany him, she had refused, saying that married people should not talk to outsiders about their personal problems.

Obviously very angry, Brett opened the session by saying that his mother-in-law was destroying his marriage. He then discussed in great detail the many ways in which Cher permitted herself to be manipulated by her mother into doing things which were destructive to the marriage.

Although her mother lived eighty-five miles away, Cher talked to her at least three to four times each week by phone. In addition, Cher insisted on going to her mother's house every weekend. When Brett refused to accompany her, she accused him of treating her mother unfairly.

Aware that Cher and her mother were close before he married her, Brett said that he had felt things would change after they were married and Cher had her own family. Even on the honeymoon, however, Cher had demanded that they return two days early after her mother had called and complained of missing her daughter.

After their son was born, she had taken him with her each time she visited her mother. Not only did Brett resent having to go himself, he felt that the visits were harmful to their son since his grandmother refused to let him out of her sight or to play with the other children in the neighborhood. He also accused her of interfering with any attempt they made to discipline the child in her presence, and said that she often countermanded their instructions to her grandson. If Brett attempted to discuss the possible undesirable effects on their son of the weekly visits, Cher would respond that it would be cruel to deprive a grandmother of the opportunity to see her only grandchild.

When they had difficulty paying the phone bill in successive months due to her numerous calls to her mother, Cher had promised to cut down to one a week. Her mother had called, however, crying and accusing her daughter of no longer caring for her. When her mother agreed to pay the phone bill, Cher quickly resumed the calls. On other occasions Cher's mother, not satisfied with just weekend visits from her daughter, would call urging Cher to come home during the week. If Cher seemed reluctant about coming, her mother would begin to cry and had on more than one occasion hinted that she might kill herself. Many times—sometimes even in the middle of the night—she had called complaining of some illness or of the fear that she was about to have a heart attack. Although Cher had herself admitted that her mother used such tactics to lure her home, she always went, saying that she could never forgive herself if something went wrong. Even her mother's doctor's attempts to assure Cher that her mother was in good health were to no avail.

Having refused to come in for the first session, Cher came for the second session with the explanation that she wanted to tell her side of the story. Although she agreed when Brett referred to her mother as a master manipulator, Cher indicated that she could not deny her mother's requests since she was her only child and all she had left after her husband had died five years earlier. The few times she had tried to stand up to her mother, she reported, she had felt so guilty that she could not eat or sleep. Although she could understand some of Brett's resentment, she was adamant in her view that he could at least go with her to visit her mother, since her mother's feelings were hurt by his absence.

Insisting that she loved both her husband and her mother, Cher said that she was being pulled apart by the two most important people in her life. Despite her husband's threats of divorce unless some changes were made, Cher said that if it ever came to that, she could never turn her back on her mother. Furthermore, she could not understand how Brett could do so either, since her mother had been very generous to them financially and had even bought them the house they now lived in. When Brett responded that he regretted ever accepting money from Cher's mother and accused her of withholding money or gifts whenever things did not go her way, Cher again agreed that her mother could and often did resort to such practices. Even after such an admission, however, Cher continued to insist that things would go along a lot smoother if Brett would be nicer to her mother and just learn to ignore such behavior.

When the counselor attempted to reflect the extreme to which Cher went in giving in to her mother's manipulative behavior, Cher again confessed that her mother was unreasonable but quickly followed up with the statement, "She is still my mother, right or wrong, and I would never intentionally do anything to hurt her as I did to my father." When questioned as to what she meant by hurting her father, Cher replied that her father might still be alive today "if I had been a more attentive daughter," and even went so far as to blame herself for being out on a date with Brett the night her father died.

She concluded the session by saying that as much as she loved Brett, if he could not understand and accept the feelings she had for her parents, then he would just have to go ahead and file for divorce.

Discussion

Despite the fact that marriage involves leaving the childhood home and creating a new home with a spouse, most couples maintain strong ties with parents, siblings, and other close relatives. Even in those cases similar to the one discussed above (Brett was fully aware before marriage of Cher's unwillingness to separate from her mother), many individuals go ahead and marry with the rationalization that they are marrying the individual and not the family.

While there are couples who sever almost all earlier family ties, very few do. Most do not even have a desire to do so, nor in most cases is it necessary even to recommend such a drastic step.

It is important, however, that couples realize that marriage involves a relationship with another person who has for many years been deeply involved, both physically and emotionally, with a close-knit nuclear body which has had and will have a great impact on the way the individual thinks and behaves as long as the person lives. To ignore the way in which individuals relate to parents and siblings within the family structure is inviting trouble. There is much to be learned about the ways in which a person can be expected to relate to his or her spouse and their own children by observing similar sorts of relationships within the spouse's family.

Tragically for all involved, Brett failed to heed the many cues which should have warned him of trouble in this respect when he choose Cher as his mate.

At birth the process of separating oneself from parents and becoming an individual begins. A long and sometimes tortuous venture, the process is nonetheless necessary if responsible and mature adults are to emerge and eventually marry and have children of their own.

Unfortunately, for many the process reaches a certain point and then comes to a grinding halt. When this occurs the person remains fixated at a certain level which can, as in the case of Cher and Brett, create problems which make married life almost impossible.

Cher's mother, like too many parents, was especially skilful in the art of manipulation. Parents often use money, gifts, threats, illness, guilt, or pity to maintain control of their children. While there are parents who contribute financially and otherwise to the support of their married children without any strings attached, it was obvious that this was not the case with Cher's mother.

Although there are marriages which manage to survive when one or both partners still maintains the small-child dependency type of relationship with his or her parents, doing so is most difficult. Sons and daughters who continue to succumb to obvious manipulative tactics are not only doing themselves a serious disservice but encouraging and reinforcing unhealthy behavior in their parents as well.

Frequently viewed by outsiders as real love and total allegiance, such relationships are often instead manifestations of rejection, lack of love, and guilt. Over-protective parents, hovering constantly over their children, may in reality be resentful parents who are overcompensating for guilt feelings generated by their lack of desire to be parents. Likewise, children who seem to be totally devoted to their parents, to the neglect of their own spouse and children, may also be trying to compensate for feelings of resentment or hatred which they cannot express to the demanding parent.

Males and females who are old enough to consider marriage seriously and who are still involved in a relationship with parents similar to the one between Cher and her mother should be viewed as bad marriage risks. While it is possible for persons to change, couples frequently come to marriage counselors for assistance with this type of problem. Since they have been locked into such a dependent way of relating to their parents for so many years, however, such individuals are very resistant to change. Consequently, many of these marriages fail when the less dependent partner insists that his or her spouse assume the role of mature husband or wife that he or she has a right to expect.

marry someone who insists on being together all the time

Midge, a twenty-nine-year-old mother and housewife, came in for counseling after her husband Ike had told her the previous evening that the marriage was over. After seven years of marriage and three children, Midge said that she had been shattered by Ike's unexpected revelation, but that she did not feel she had any right to stand in his way if a separation was what he really wanted.

Despite her apparent willingness to give him up, Midge stated that she still loved Ike and did not want a divorce. Finally admitting that she had been aware that he was not completely happy in the marriage, Midge said that she had thought that Ike would stay married to her because of her total devotion to him if for no other reason.

In an attempt to explain her undying allegiance to Ike, Midge revealed that she had been reared in a family in which oneness and unity in marriage had always been stressed, with emphasis on total commitment of the wife to the husband. Though there had been times when it had been difficult to go along with some of her husband's ideas, Midge indicated that she still believed in the basic philosophy that the husband was the head of the family and the wife's major responsibility was that of providing support in the husband's struggle for fulfillment. When some of her friends had questioned the wisdom of such an outlook, Midge had replied that she viewed her husband's successes as her own and that she was perfectly content to remain in the background and let him reap the more visible rewards.

Although Midge continued in the first session to insist that, if necessary, she was willing to sacrifice her happiness for that of her husband, she was more openly embittered in the second session after a week in which her husband had been even more emphatic about wanting a separation. After she again described how she had put him first in everything to the point of giving up her friends, quitting school herself to earn enough for his education, cooking and washing till all hours of the night, always listening when he needed a shoulder to cry on, never voicing her opinions or discussing her problems, Midge said tearfully that she was now being cast aside like an old shoe.

When she had gathered the courage to talk with Ike about her hurt over being abandoned after being so faithful and sharing his dreams for so many years, he had said that he had grown to see her as a millstone around his neck. While he had grown professionally and socially, she had remained still. Rather than pursuing her own interests, she seemed to have attached herself to him like a parasite. She always wanted them to do everything together. While he had been flattered by her devotion and willingness to sacrifice her beliefs and interests for him in the earlier stages of their relationship, Ike said that he had begun to feel stifled and resentful as a result of her constant insistence on oneness and togetherness.

Although Ike agreed that she had been responsible for much of the success he had enjoyed, Midge admitted that she had been devastated when he had told her that he found other women much more challenging and exciting to be around. While providing support and closeness when needed, they maintained a separateness, and Ike said he found them refreshing compared to Midge, who was always underfoot, agreeing with him on every issue. When Ike had tried to explain to Midge his need for distance in the relationship as opposed to doing everything as a team and always maintaining total harmony, Midge had accused him of forsaking their marriage vows and condoning a split which no marriage could long endure.

Discussion

While unity and commitment to a life together are essential in a good marriage, too much togetherness can spell disaster. Although Biblical writers refer to marriage as a relationship in which two people "become one," this should not be interpreted to mean that all individuality is lost in marriage. Nowhere is the uniqueness and worth of every human being stressed more than in the Bible.

Although the need for independence, privacy, and individuality may vary from individual to individual, a good marriage encourages the never-ending quest for self-actualization and self-realization for each partner. As paradoxical as it may sound, separateness in a relationship tends to build a desire for more togetherness; distance, a greater desire for closeness.

Although some people seem satisfied to sacrifice their personal identity, dreams, goals, and aspirations for those of their mate, most would eventually find such a relationship unbearable. When a person is called on to make such a sacrifice, it means that certain powerful and significant personal needs will forever remain unfulfilled. While marriage always demands that we give up something to get something, it is appalling to think of the price we have paid in human suffering because of our allegiance to the concept that if marriage is to succeed, one partner, usually the female, must be willing to submit to a life of self-denial.

Under such conditions even the spouse who maintains the dominant or superior position will grow to resent intrusions into his or her privacy by the weaker spouse who insists that he or she be permitted to live the life of an ever-present and compliant servant, totally dedicated to the development of the more assertive spouse.

There are those who would argue that the emphasis on personal growth and individuality in marriage is contrary to the teaching of unity and oneness in marriage. Others would argue that emphasis on personal growth and achievement for both husband and wife would play havoc with the more traditional view that the husband should be the head of the household. It is not our purpose to resolve such issues. Indeed, we are not concerned with who should be dominant or submissive, inferior or superior. We are instead concerned with the right of individuals to strive for self-realization. As stated elsewhere, it is necessary to love and respect oneself before love for another can become a reality in any true sense of the word. And one cannot learn to love and respect oneself unless encouraged to live in a manner which enables him or her to utilize God-given abilities and talents. Persons who are permitted to do so feel much better about themselves and subsequently find themselves able to enter into a close personal relationship with another human being willing to extend to them the same freedom.

For many couples the balance between the needs for togetherness and separateness is almost impossible to assess while they are dating. This is due to the feeling shared by many couples in love: they cannot get enough of each other. Although such feelings are quite common, most couples eventually come down to earth and realize that life demands that all human beings face life first and last as individuals. No matter how close two people may become in marriage, John will always be John, and Mary will always be Mary.

While the needs for togetherness and separateness will vary from couple to couple, those contemplating marriage would do well to raise some of the following questions.

(1) How much freedom am I allowed to be my own person?
(2) Am I encouraged to pursue my own interests, or am I always expected to relegate my interests to a secondary position?
(3) Are my needs considered important by the other person?
(4) Does the other person seem threatened if I express interest in a career of my own?
(5) Does the other person insist that we do everything together?
(6) Does he or she get upset if I want to be alone or do things with other people sometimes?
(7) Is he or she excessively possessive or jealous?
(8) Are my wishes and opinions respected and given reasonable consideration?
(9) Do I frequently feel smothered and stifled by the other person's presence?
(10) Do I frequently resent the demands placed on me by the other person?
(11) Do I feel that the other person's requests and demands on me are reasonable?

(12) Has the other person made it clear what he or she expects my role in the relationship to be?

(13) Would he or she be able to accept and love me if I should change my mind in the future?

(14) Does the other person so completely dominate my life that I feel like a big zero when we're apart?

(15) Am I dependent on the other person for meaning and purpose in life?

While it is true that expectations will vary from couple to couple as to what they expect from their mates in marriage, the need for tolerance and acceptance of the other person as a unique and worthwhile individual cannot be overemphasized. If the freedom to develop as an individual is lacking in a relationship prior to marriage, then it is apt to be lacking after marriage. It has been our observation that the absence of growth as individuals leads to an absence of growth as a couple. Although there is always the danger that a couple will grow apart if individual development is encouraged, the danger is much greater if it is not encouraged.

While the loss of individual identity can be a major source of distress in marriage, it can be a tragedy if the relationship is terminated for any reason. A young man said recently, "If anything happened to my girlfriend, I would have nothing to live for." On another occasion an older woman said after learning that her husband had a terminal illness, "I am so dependent on him for everything and my life is so wrapped up in his that I will not know which way to turn after he is gone."

The loss of a loved one is for most people a time of great sadness and loneliness. The tragedy is compounded when the person left feels that he or she has lost all sense of personal identity as a result of the termination of the relationship. This tends to happen when one partner in the relationship is required to devote himself or herself to the other so completely that all sense of self is drowned in a sea of oneness and togetherness.

marry someone because you "have to get married"

Nan and Leif had been married for seven years and had one six-year-old daughter, Amy. They came for counseling because of a difference of opinion regarding Nan's desire to go back to school. Leif opposed such a move, saying that Nan should stay at home with their daughter.

In discussing their earlier relationship, Nan told the counselor that they had started dating when she was 15 and Leif 16. They both had attended the same high school. They had "gone steady," and neither had had much experience dating prior to their meeting in the tenth grade.

After dating almost three years, Nan said, she became pregnant and they "had to get married." She had been opposed to the marriage from the beginning because, she said, she was just not ready to be a wife and mother. She had even gone so far as to consider abortion. Although he had not planned to get married so early, Leif said that he loved Nan and was excited when she told him she was going to have a baby. He admitted that it had been all he could do to persuade her to forget the abortion and get married.

Agreeing with Leif that the decision had been a difficult one for her, Nan said that she had consented to go ahead with the marriage because she loved Leif and believed abortion to be wrong. On the other hand, she said that she resented being pregnant and having to get married at such a young age when she had so many things she still wanted to do. She had hoped that her resentment would lessen and that she would gradually adjust to being married, but Nan said that instead her resentment had grown to include her daughter as well as her husband. While she would have perferred to be out dating, traveling, or just enjoying life, she found herself staying home to clean the house and change diapers. Her pregnancy had ended all plans for a career in journalism, Nan concluded, at least for the foreseeable future.

Not only had she felt bad about the pregnancy; after the birth of her child her guilt had increased as she grew to see herself as a poor mother. Leif agreed with Nan's assessment of herself as a mother, acknowledging that she spent a minimum of time with Amy and seemed to resent having to do even this much. Both agreed that Amy had suffered from the tension between them and was confused as a result of their many disagreements about how she should be reared and disciplined.

In recent months their dissatisfaction with each other had grown, and both reported that they were now fighting over the way Nan cooked and kept house. Leif said with considerable fervor that Nan acted upset if he asked her to do anything around the house. Rather than going through all the hassle, he said, he had taken to doing many of the household chores himself. Even this had not seemed to placate Nan, however.

Regarding her desire to go back to school, Nan said that she was not cut out to be a housewife and wanted a career of her own. While a career would not make up for all she had lost as a result of marrying so young, she felt that it would help. Although still a young woman, she said that she was not getting any younger and that life was passing her by.

While she managed to contain her anger and resentment most of the time, Nan confessed that it became much harder to do when she saw friends who had waited until they were older to get married and have children going off to Europe or living in more luxurious surroundings. When she saw so many other girls doing the things she had wanted to do before settling down, Nan said she realized just how much she had missed. At these times in particular she found the thought of marriage so restrictive that she could hardly bear the idea of staying married another day.

When Leif attempted to discuss the love he still had for Nan and Amy, Nan quickly interrupted to say that despite all his talk of love, he had not been ready for marriage either. Although she admitted Leif had adjusted better than she had, Nan said that he had never made enough money to support a family and that consequently they lived under constant stress. When Leif defended himself by saying that he had been a loving husband and father, Nan agreed but said, "You cannot live on love alone."

Discussion

An unwanted pregnancy is a difficult problem at best. Making a decision about it to please someone else is an additional burden, and if that decision is "having to get married," the outcome can often be disastrous. Nan and Leif's feelings and marital problems are common for couples who feel they "had to get married." Nan and Leif have accumulated resentments, guilt, anger, and stress and at this point will have to deal with the situation they have now as a result of feeling the pressure to get married at such an early age. But what could other couples do when faced with the same dilemma at a young age or at any age?

Many couples who care for each other express their affection through sexual relations. Whether we like it or not, this is a fact of life. However, many couples who engage in intercourse are not prepared to get married or raise a child which may be born as a result of their sexual expression. The availability of birth control devices makes untimely marriage and unwanted pregnancy unnecessary. The fact is that pregnancy can occur the very first time a man and woman have intercourse. Many people are ignorant of this fact or decide to "take a chance." Others are embarrassed to seek medical advice about birth control or go to a drugstore and purchase birth control devices. Still others experience conflicting feelings about intercourse and take the risk of getting pregnant instead of coming to grips with their feelings. If Nan and Leif could look back, they might reflect that the effort to use birth control would have been a minor obstacle in comparison to the struggles they are experiencing seven years later. While the use of contraceptives is for many a moral issue, an unwanted child is also a moral issue of utmost importance.

Most of the previous discussion has focused on Nan's pregnancy as the major factor in her decision to marry. We have discussed the issue of pregnancy because of the astounding number of girls and women who are already pregnant when they marry.

It is not the purpose of this book to go into the moral questions involved in the issue of premarital sex. The fact remains, however, that thousands of young people do engage in sex before marriage and many pregnancies result. For most individuals an unwanted pregnancy is traumatic. For many abortion is immoral. Bringing an unwanted child into this world is, for some, even more immoral. Either decision often results in grief, depression, guilt, anger, or resentment, and these feelings may not be resolved for years.

Some couples like Nan and Leif, who decided to go ahead with marriage, are never able to overcome their resentment for "having to get married." Many couples, even after ten or fifteen years of marriage, come in for counseling still bitter and resentful that they married under such conditions.

While we have discussed premarital pregnancies as a major factor in many problem marriages, it is important to realize that other causes or pressures may prompt individuals to marry before they are ready to assume the responsibilities of marriage. For example, parents have been known to push their children into an early marriage, sometimes deliberately, sometimes unknowingly. Or one partner may continue to pressure the other to marry before he or she is ready.

Whatever the reason for early or premature marriage in which one or both partners is not ready for marriage, the results can be disastrous. While the divorce rate is high for couples who marry at any age, the percentage of teenage marriages which end in divorce is exceedingly so. To be pressured into marriage before one is ready—at any age for any reason—is to invite trouble.

ignore family planning until pregnancy occurs

"I'm pregnant and I don't know what to do, but I think I want an abortion," Michele tearfully told the counselor. She went on, "Michael and I have been married a year and a half, but we're not ready to have children. I know I'm not ready. I haven't finished college and I won't be twenty-one until next month. Michael's twenty-two, but he's only been out of school a year, and he's having problems with his job. We're having problems too, and a baby wouldn't make them any better. I'd been taking the pill, but the doctor took me off it for a few months, and I hadn't been using anything else. I didn't think I could get pregnant right after going off the pill. Anyway, I don't think I should have a baby when there are already problems in our marriage. Of course our parents would never forgive us if they knew we were thinking about an abortion. They want grandchildren and would help us out if we decided to have the baby, but I still don't think going through with the pregnancy would be the best thing for us or the baby right now."

"Michele's right," Michael added. "I thought I'd feel good if she got pregnant when she went off the pill, but when she did, it was sort of a shock. We've been fighting a lot the last several months. I hate my job but took it so Michele could finish her last year of school here. We never seem to have enough money, and I just can't face having a baby right now. The thing is, though, that the idea of abortion really bothers me. I had a strict religious upbringing, and before this pregnancy happened to us I was totally against abortion. Now that we're faced with having a baby we didn't plan, I'm not so sure about my feelings. I'm really confused."

Mary and Richard, both twenty-six, looked older and already seemed sad about their lives. "I feel like I'm falling apart at the seams," Mary began in their first session with the marriage counselor. "We're both trying to finish our Ph.D.'s. I have almost completed my research, but with housework, cooking, and taking care of our four-year-old daughter, I can't handle it anymore. It's no problem for Richard. He can go to his office at night and work, and he doesn't have to worry about the dishes, the laundry, or Laura. It doesn't seem fair. I'm pulled in so many directions that sometimes I feel like I'll crack open if I have to endure one more frustration. Richard is a good husband, but I really don't think he understands the amount of responsibility I feel I have. We both planned and wanted to go to graduate school when we were married right out of college, but we didn't plan Laura. She came seven months after we were married. She's a good child—a delight—but sometimes I feel like I'm getting old before I've gotten anywhere in life."

Discussion

Child-rearing requires much emotional and physical energy. In our experience with married couples, it is clear that a child who is planned and wanted can enhance a marriage, while one who is unplanned and unwanted can place a great burden on a couple. Marriage requires many adjustments, particularly in the first few years. The kind of relationship a man and woman establish during courtship and the initial years of marriage will set the tone for many years to come. Unplanned children can and do create anxieties which are often never entirely resolved.

When one considers that rearing a child consumes twenty or more years of a couple's life, it would seem obvious that the decision to have a baby requires thought and planning. However, Michele and Michael's and Mary and Richard's situation are all too common. Therefore, we cannot overemphasize how important it is for couples contemplating marriage to discuss their feelings and plans regarding children in their proposed marriage.

Some important questions for such discussions are:
(1) Do we agree about birth control and the use of contraceptive measures?
(2) What would we do if an unplanned pregnancy occurred?
(3) Do we both want children?

(4) If so, can we agree on the number and the time?

(5) If children are not wanted, do we agree on this?

(6) Do we generally agree about child-rearing practices?

(7) Are our family goals reasonably compatible?

(8) Is there pressure from family members to have or not to have children? If so, how do we handle it?

If couples are unable to agree in their answers to these questions, problems can easily erupt later. It is a serious mistake to assume that any differences can be worked out after marriage, as many unhappy couples can attest.

marry someone with whom you are obviously sexually incompatible

Yancy and Billy Joe opened the first counseling session, as many couples do, with the complaint they were having sexual problems. Frustrated and hurt by Bill Joe's unwillingness to have sex more than once every two weeks, Yancy said she could accept this if she really believed it was due to a difference in their sex drives. Admitting that she already had a low opinion of herself physically due to Billy Joe's criticism of her small breasts and slender, almost boyish build, Yancy said that his behavior only served to convince her that she was indeed sexually unattractive to her husband.

Yancy ignored Billy Joe's attempts to convince her that he found her more attractive when she weighed more. Persisting in his attempts to get his point across, Billy Joe said, "I like my women with some meat on their bones." Both mentioned that Yancy had lost twenty pounds since their marriage. Yancy explained the weight loss by saying that she preferred the "Twiggy" look because she not only looked better but also felt better.

In an attempt to please her husband, Yancy said, she had gained fifteen pounds the previous year but had soon lost it because she felt so uncomfortable. Even when she weighed more, however, she insisted there had been so significant change in Billy Joe's sexual interest. Agreeing with her, Billy Joe said that the only conclusion he could come up with, after racking his brain for months, was that he just did not have as strong a sex drive as his wife. When we attempted to explore other possible underlying causes for their lack of sexual satisfaction, both Billy Joe and Yancy insisted they had a good marriage, were well pleased with each other, and had lots of fun.

Discussion

One of the most frequent complaints couples express in counseling is the partners' differences regarding the desire and frequency of sexual intercourse. Some men complain that their
wives never really seem to be interested in sex but only go
through the motions because they feel obligated. Women often
respond by accusing their husbands of being sex maniacs who
want to have intercourse every night. One woman recently said
that her husband interpreted as an invitation to go to bed anything she did to be affectionate. Commenting that he could not
understand that there were times when she just wanted to be
held, she went on to say that she had learned to dread any kind of
contact, lest her husband misinterpret her intentions.

Until fairly recently most of the complaints regarding a partner's lack of sexual interest seemed to come from males. While
many men still complain of this, women are increasingly expressing a lack of sexual fulfillment in marriage. It is no longer uncommon to hear a wife say that her sex drive must be much
greater than her husband's and that she would like to have sex
more often.

No matter who the initiator is, most individuals, both men
and women, feel it is a real put-down if their partner says no
when sex is suggested. Most couples manage to handle rejection
fairly well in other areas of interpersonal relationships. Not so
with sex. To be refused when sexual overtures are made is for
most people the ultimate in rejection. Some take it so hard that
they sulk or pout for days. One woman recently responded to her
husband's criticism that she had never taken the initiative sexually in their five years of marriage: "I've never forgotten the night
shortly after our marriage when I asked you to make love to me
and you refused. I said then I'd never ask you again, and I
haven't."

Despite the so-called sexual revolution, couples like Billy Joe
and Yancy continue in increasing numbers to complain of
difficulties and a lack of satisfaction in their sexual relationships.
It appears that more people are engaging in sex but enjoying it

less than ever before in our history. While there is no way to prove or disprove such a claim, it does appear that more couples are being counseled for sex-related difficulties than in any previous generation. Indeed, few counseling sessions with couples fail to bring out sexual concerns in some form or another.

Evidence of the burgeoning number of sexual complaints can be found in the popularity of sex clinics in this country in recent years. It has been estimated that there are in this country at least five thousand clinics which deal solely with sexual problems. Of the many problems seen in such clinics, those stemming from couples' differences in sexual energy and interest abound. Many couples ask, "How often should we have sexual relations?" "What is the average number of times per week for other couples our age?" "What is normal?" The last two questions are practically unanswerable—no one really knows. The answer to the first question is simple: whenever both partners are willing and conditions permit. The only real issue in the matter of frequency is reasonable compatibility. If some couples want to have sex once a year and can agree on the time, then why make it an issue? If other couples want to have sex twice a day and can agree on the timing, who is to say that they have a problem? If, however, one partner wants to have sex three times a week while the other is satisfied with three times a month, then there is obviously the potential for problems.

This should not be interpreted to mean that any partners will always want to have sex at the same time. Every person should have the right to say no without the other person feeling crushed. After all, only machines should be expected to perform whenever they are called on to do so, and even machines sometimes fail to perform according to expectations. If individuals—either male or female—do not have the right to say no, then the times when they say yes become meaningless. Regarding sexual requests, to do less than to reserve for oneself the right to say yes or no and to honor the same in one's partner is at best dehumanizing. At worst it can be painful and destructive.

Most couples experience sexual difficulties of some kind at some time in their marriage. Many of these problems are mild and temporary, and most couples never seek professional help for sexual dysfunctioning. In some cases, however, sexual problems may be the only outward manifestation of more serious problems. Despite their claims that they had a good marriage, it is very possible that Billy Joe and Yancy's problems were more than just a difference in the intensity or frequency of their sexual needs. On the other hand, the complaint is heard so often that it cannot be ignored as a major problem among couples. Partners do have differing levels of sexual energy and interest, and this can lead to serious problems in some marriages.

Since such differences can lead to conflict in marriage, it is advisable to learn as much as possible about one's intended spouse and his or her sexual inclinations and needs. For those who place no restraints on sexual activities prior to marriage, this may seem to be a simple task. Even under these conditions, however, initial impressions can be deceiving. Some people may, for example, seem to have insatiable sexual needs while dating. After the novelty or excitement of a new partner begins to decline, these same individuals may display a noticeable lack of sexual interest in their spouses. On the other hand, the person who may at first appear to be shy and inhibited may blossom into a person of great sexual passion once certain inhibitions are overcome.

If, however, one's intended spouse shows an aversion for or an almost total lack of interest in sexual matters, this should alert the partner to the possible existence of sexual attitudes which may be hard to change. If there is a noticeable difference in sexual needs in regard to strength or frequency, this also should not be ignored.

Again a word of caution is in order. Many young and sexually inexperienced females do not seem to possess the sometimes almost overpowering need for sex felt by young men of a similar age. Whether these differences are due to psychological or physiological reasons may be debated. Nevertheless, they seem to exist in a significant number of young couples who seek counseling.

Couples may be sexually incompatible in ways other than

frequency or strength of needs. They may, for example, differ greatly in the ways they choose to satisfy their sexual needs. Sexual activities which may be considered enjoyable and normal by one spouse may seem unpleasant, disgusting, or even perverted to his or her partner. Other differences which can cause problems in marriage are such sex-related questions as methods of birth control, number of children desired, and views on abortion.

While it is not the purpose of this book to deal with the many social and moral issues centered on sex, it cannot be emphasized too strongly that before marriage couples should exert maximum effort in the exploration and resolution of the many differences and issues related to sexual practices and beliefs. If such matters are ignored prior to marriage, then controversy at a later date might well destroy the couple's chances for a successful marriage.

marry someone who encourages sexual involvement with others after marriage

Leta and Stan had married each other with the understanding that they would not be restricted in regard to their relationships with other men and women. Although they had both had sexual relations with others before they met, they said that they had had no desire or need to get involved with anyone else in the six months they dated. During the first year of their marriage they still had not been sexually involved with anyone else, although they had talked about it on numerous occasions, and each still agreed that the other could become involved with someone else if the desire or opportunity arose.

In the second year of their marriage, however, Stan had begun to talk more frequently of being attracted to women in the office where he worked. Much to her surprise, Leta felt pangs of jealousy when Stan told her that he had taken Sue, one of his secretaries, out to lunch. She continued to insist, however, that Stan was free to do as he pleased. Within the next month Stan had three dates with Sue and had sexual intercourse with her twice. When he told Leta of his sexual relationship with Sue, Leta was infuriated. Despite Leta's anger, however, Stan announced his intention of continuing the relationship, reminding Leta of the agreement they had made before marriage.

Two months later at a large dinner party, Jeff, one of Stan's business partners, had asked Leta to dance. Aware of the arrangement which Leta and Stan had, Jeff asked her to meet him the following afternoon for a drink. Although she had still not dated anyone since her marriage to Stan, Leta found Jeff attractive and agreed to the meeting. When he suggested they have sex the next day, she had agreed. Later, in discussing her decision with a counselor, Leta said that she had gone to bed with Jeff not only because she found him attractive, but also to get back at Stan.

In the third year of their marriage the pattern continued; both Leta and Stan became involved with still other men and women on a casual basis. One night, after both had had too much to drink, Stan suggested that they invite Jeff and Sue to come over and all go to bed together. Although she had felt uncomfortable with the idea, Leta had given in when Stan persisted. Sue was out of town, but Jeff had accepted the invitation. While admitting that she felt strange about being in bed with two men at the same time, Leta confessed that she had also found it exciting. On another occasion they invited Sue over for dinner and the three of them ended up in bed together. In the next two months Leta and Stan became involved with another married couple and switched partners on several occasions. Twice they had all gone to bed together.

In the latter part of the third year of their marriage, Leta became pregnant. While admitting that she had found some of the sexual encounters with others exciting, Leta said that she had never felt right about such activities. Upon discovering that she was pregnant, she had immediately informed Stan that she felt such behavior would be inappropriate for the parents of a small child. At first vigorously protesting Leta's demand that he also give up all sexual involvement outside the marriage, Stan had eventually promised to do so when Leta threatened not to have the baby unless he did.

When Stan informed Sue of his promise the next day, she had suggested that they meet on their lunch hour without telling Leta. Readily agreeing to the arrangement, Stan managed to keep his meetings with Sue from Leta for several months. While Leta was in the hospital for the birth of the baby, however, someone informed her that they had seen Stan entering Sue's apartment one night after hospital visiting hours were over. When she left the hospital, Leta contacted a lawyer and filed for divorce. It was at this point that Stan persuaded her to see a marriage counselor with him.

In the sessions which followed, both Leta and Stan admitted that they had felt jealous when the other had been with another man or woman for sexual purposes. Stan said that the thought of

Leta with another man aroused in him strong feelings of in-adequacy as a male. Expressing similar sentiments, Leta said that if she had been an adequate wife, Stan would never have needed to go elsewhere for sexual satisfaction.

In spite of their frankness with each other and Stan's promises that he would not engage in such behavior again, Leta continued to express doubts about his sincerity, saying that she did not know if she could ever trust him again.

Three months later, still saying they loved each other, Leta and Stan were divorced.

Discussion

Despite all the recent talk of the sexual revolution and of sexual freedom in marriage, most couples would find an ar-rangement such as that agreed on by Leta and Stan impossible to live with. No matter how liberated the couple may appear or how much they verbalize their willingness to permit each other to have sexual contacts with others, either one or both of the mar-riage partners usually ends up being hurt if this is carried out. Despite the popularity of books dealing with the relaxation of all sexual restraints and philosophies which encourage the freedom of individuals to express all dimensions of their feelings, if put into practice these can and often do lead to disaster for individu-als and couples. While it may sound good to talk of total free-dom to express any feelings one has, the married person who ex-presses bisexual or homosexual feelings or the need for group sexual encounters may be indulging in an honest expression of his or her feelings but inviting disaster in the marriage relation-ship.

There are many differing opinions as to why practices such as group sex, wife-swapping, open marriage, and bed-hopping have become so popular in recent years. Explanations range from sheer boredom with one's spouse to emotional instability. Some suggest such practices are indicative of a fear of intimacy and closeness in a one-to-one relationship. Individuals going from one conquest to another may be trying to prove something about their masculinity or femininity, or to prove that they are sophisticated and open-minded about sexual matters. Still others say it is just the spirit of our times and is indicative of a more open and wholesome approach to sex.

Whatever the causes, most individuals cannot endure the thought of someone they love being sexually involved with another person. Those who boast of the ability to do so may be saying more about the quality and depth of their love than they are about their sexual liberation. Despite opinions to the contrary, our work with couples has led us to conclude that sexual involvement outside marriage will shake most marriages to the roots and is almost always detrimental to the development of a good marital relationship.

While some would say that we see only the people who experience problems with such an arrangement, we have seen the problem enough to suggest that couples anticipating marriage ask themselves the following questions.

(1) How do we each feel about sexual exclusiveness in marriage?
(2) How would I feel if my husband or wife had sexual relations with someone else?
(3) What does sex mean to us as a part of our marital relationship?
(4) How are we going to handle feelings of sexual attraction either of us may have for someone outside our marriage?
(5) How are we going to behave regarding sexual exclusiveness in our marriage?
(6) How are we going to deal with invitations from others to engage in extramarital sexual relations or flirtations?

While there are those who insist that their marriages have been enriched by extramarital relationships, it cannot be emphasized too strongly that this issue should be examined thoroughly by the couple contemplating marriage. If either partner even hints that sexual involvement with others can be expected, then it is our suggestion that marriage to this person be re-evaluated and approached with caution.

marry someone who is sexually unresponsive

After several minutes of chit-chat, Natalie, a twenty-three-year-old fashion designer, told the marriage counselor that she had to talk with someone about her lack of sexual desire before she lost her husband or her mind.

When the counselor tried to reassure Natalie that it was not uncommon for women her age to experience times in which they had no desire to have sex with their husbands, Natalie responded by saying, "But what if you feel this way most of the time?"

Referring to herself as a frigid woman, Natalie said that she loved her husband more than anything in the world and wanted nothing more than to please him sexually. Not only did she want to satisfy her husband sexually; she added, with considerable resentment, that she saw herself as being less than a complete woman and felt that she was missing out on something she ought to be enjoying. "I hear and read of all these other women and their fantastic sexual experiences, and I feel cheated because I am unable to share such experiences with someone I love. I know there must be something wrong with me. At other times I resent the pleasure my husband gets out of sex because I feel so frustrated by the whole thing. Sometimes I get so frustrated that I am tempted to go to bed with another man just to see if I am capable of responding sexually to any man."

In discussing her previous sexual experiences, Natalie said that she had never had intercourse with anyone but her husband. "I always expected to be a virgin when I married." Although she had always believed that it was wrong to have sex before marriage, Natalie said that she had agreed to go ahead and go to bed with Russ because "I convinced myself that it was not wrong to have sex if you really loved the person."

In discussing her premarital sexual relations further, Natalie said that while she had enjoyed it to a degree, especially the affection and foreplay, she had never had an orgasm. She attributed this to the guilt she felt about having sex before marriage and convinced herself that things would improve after marriage, when she would no longer be plagued by guilt feelings.

When asked about the sexual attitudes in her family, Natalie said that when she was a child her parents had never discussed sex with her and seemed embarrassed whenever the subject was brought up. "Although no one ever told me that sex was wrong or dirty," Natalie said, "somehow it was never communicated to me that it was normal and desirable either."

Returning to her relationship with her husband, Natalie said that instead of getting better after marriage, her sexual difficulties had increased to the point that she could now hardly stand to have her husband touch her. When he made sexual advances, she usually excused her lack of desire by saying that she was too tired or had too many things on her mind. If she did force herself to go ahead and make love despite her lack of interest, her attitude was usually "Let's get it over with as soon as possible." Even when she felt the infrequent desire to make love, Natalie reported that she could enjoy the foreplay up to a certain point, and then she would freeze up. "No matter how hard I try, the orgasm just won't come," she said.

Natalie indicated that on those occasions, although she allowed her husband to continue until he ejaculated, she felt completely numb and had often found it physically painful to continue. The few times she began to feel sexually aroused, she would say to herself, "This time it is going to happen." On each occasion, however, she had felt the pleasant sensations crowded out by old doubts and fears.

Natalie confessed that for the first year of their marriage she had been so convinced that there was something wrong with her sexually that she had faked orgasm so that Russ would not suspect that his wife was abnormal. The tension and frustration had become so great after the first year, however, that she had finally told Russ that she was not experiencing orgasm or receiving any great pleasure from sexual intercourse. Although he had been crushed by his wife's confession, Russ had attributed the absence of pleasure to her lack of experience and attempted to persuade her that everything would work out in the near future. When things had not improved after several months, however, Russ began to blame himself for his wife's failure to enjoy sex. As a result, both Natalie and Russ had grown to feel sexually inadequate. Things had become so bad by the time she came to see the counselor that both Russ and Natalie now approached bedtime with dread. Natalie reported that many nights, long after Russ had fallen asleep, she lay awake crying over her sexual failures. Because of the tension generated at bedtime, Russ had begun to stay up to watch the late show or read until he was certain that Natalie was asleep.

Discussion

Natalie is typical of the many women, both younger and older, who complain that they seldom or never experience orgasm during sexual intercourse with their husbands. Despite the current emphasis in our society on sexual freedom and pleasure for women, there are still many who have never known what it is to have an orgasm. Indeed, the lack of sexual fulfillment is discussed so often in marriage counseling that we would suspect that the situation is much more widespread than some of the studies dealing with it would lead us to believe.

In any review of the literature about sex, couples who are experiencing sexual problems or doubts should remember that books and magazines are written to be sold. Editors are aware that publications dealing with sexual matters are eye-catchers. In recent years, with the publicity enjoyed by the women's movement in general and sexual concerns in particular, a whole new fertile and lucrative territory has been opened for those with an eye for profit. While many of the publications concerning female sexuality have considerable value, others have done a world of harm, either due to the authors' inadequate knowledge and training or through misinterpretation by the readers. Nowhere is this more apparent than in the area of female orgasm.

As a result of the female book and magazine market's saturation with articles emphasizing orgasm, many women have come to see themselves as abnormal or somehow less than complete women because of their lack of orgasmic experiences.

While we would not want to minimize the problem or treat the matter of female orgasm as if it were of little consequence, it is important that women (and their boyfriends and husbands) learn not to view themselves as sexual freaks because they have not achieved the fantastic sexual experiences described in so many current books and magazines.

While the absence of orgasm as well as other sexual problems can be indicative of some deep-seated and unresolved emotional conflict, most of the women concerned about their lack of sexual fulfillment are emotionally healthy individuals. Although it can be frustrating and provoke great anxiety in females (and the men involved in sexual relationships with them), it should be emphasized that in most cases the lack of orgasm is treatable and excellent results are reported by those skilled in the treatment of such difficulties. With patience and understanding, many couples are able to resolve the problem themselves, although it may not be done overnight.

If it is true that many women have difficulty reaching orgasm, how can the couple contemplating marriage determine if the problem can be resolved within a reasonable time and with reasonable effort? How can they be fairly certain that the problem will not eventually destroy their relationship?

While this may be difficult to do in some cases, there are clues which can provide some insight into the seriousness of the problem. If there is reason to suspect that the lack of orgasm and sexual pleasure may be a manifestation of more serious personality problems, the couple might want to raise some of the following questions. If the answer to any of them is yes, further examination is recommended.

(1) Does she seem to have a problem with closeness and intimacy even when sex is not a question?
(2) Does she have a problem communicating with and relating to other people in general?
(3) Does she have a tendency to withdraw or isolate herself?
(4) Does she keep her opinions and feelings to herself or under tight control at all times?

(5) Does she have a serious problem expressing feelings such as anger, love, affection, and sorrow?

(6) Is she frequently depressed for long periods of time during which she shows no interest in physical and sexual contact?

(7) Does she show other signs of being emotionally unstable (i.e., unduly suspicious, fearful, anxious, distrustful; bizarre thoughts or behavior)?

(8) Is she unable to discuss sexual matters and problems freely?

(9) Does she have great difficulty in discussing other problems openly?

(10) Does she show a willingness to seek help if problems are indicated or suspected?

(11) Does she seem repulsed by the thought of sex?

(12) Does she become upset if kissed, hugged, or petted?

(13) Does she tend to dismiss the problem with the explanation that it will go away after marriage?

(14) Does she express a lot of physical complaints or use other excuses to avoid sexual contact?

The lack of orgasm in females may be due to other less pervasive or serious causes. For example, many young women who have difficulty experiencing orgasm have never before had a lasting or intimate relationship with a man. Many have dated a variety of men but have not yet learned how to handle deep feelings of emotional and physical intimacy.

They may also be experiencing difficulties due to unrealistic expectations regarding sex. Many expect to become sexually responsive or to achieve optimum sexual functioning overnight. When this does not happen, they experience disillusionment, disappointment, and self-critical feelings which interfere with a realistic appraisal of themselves. While it is normal to want to get the most out of sex, it is unrealistic to expect American women, who have been reared in a society which has for years been sexually prohibitive for females, to respond to their sexual needs as if they had been conditioned to do so.

Many of these women, though normal and healthy in other

ways, are unfamiliar with their own bodies. Many are unaware of the sexual responses of which they are capable; many are too inhibited and embarrassed even to talk about their bodies, viewing masturbation or curiosity about their sexuality as shameful.

Many have never discussed their sexual feelings, attitudes, and experiences with anyone, including parents, friends, siblings, or even counselors. Some have never even discussed matters such as menstruation and physical changes which cause most adolescents considerable concern and adjustment.

While there are no guarantees, the chances for sexual adjustment seem considerably enhanced if the woman:

(1) is relatively healthy, both emotionally and physically.
(2) is willing to discuss problems freely and openly and to seek professional help if she has any questions.
(3) seems to have a healthy desire for physical contact.
(4) is outgoing and interested in people in general.
(5) gives and responds to love and affection with ease and comfort.
(6) is able to express other feelings openly and freely.
(7) is not unduly inhibited about sexual concerns.

While this discussion has focused on females and their sexual problems, the same suggestions would apply to women who are dating men with similar problems. If, for example, a man is impotent, a woman would do well to raise the kinds of questions listed above. While it is true that many females come to marriage counselors with sexual complaints, in recent years males have been coming in increasing numbers also, with complaints of impotence, premature ejaculation, lack of interest in sex, fears of being homosexual, and other sex-related concerns. Women no longer have a monopoly on sexual problems. Indeed, they never did.

Where sexual problems are known to exist prior to marriage, they should not be dismissed with the idea that they will take care of themselves after marriage. As too many couples can testify, they can become even more serious after marriage.

Ross had been married to Katrina for five years when he ca...
alone to see a counselor. Admitting that they were having marital
difficulties, Ross quickly stated that Katrina had not come for
counseling because the problems in their marriage were the result of his own personal problems.

Ross expressed a desire to talk about sexual feelings and said
that he was becoming increasingly less interested in having sexual relations with Katrina. In discussing the matter further, Ross
said that he had come to the conclusion, after five years of
marriage, that he really preferred sex with men. After describing
Katrina as a beautiful woman who would be considered very sexy
by most men, Ross said that he had been going out at least once a
week for the past several months looking for some male to have
sex with. Although he usually felt ashamed after these encounters and would resolve not to do the same thing again, his desire
for male companionship and sex would become so strong that
within a few days he would find himself cruising the street again
looking for a partner.

Having been aware for some time that something was wrong,
Katrina had confronted Ross some weeks earlier when, in one of
his irritable and restless moods, he had asked her to leave him
alone when she tried to embrace him. At first refusing to discuss
his problem, Ross had eventually given in and told Katrina of his
homosexual activities. When she questioned him further, he
revealed that he had been sexually involved with other males on a
fairly regular basis when he was fourteen. By the age of sixteen he
had concluded that he was gay.

Since such behavior was against his religious beliefs, and
because he felt that his parents could never accept their son's
being gay, Ross had dated a number of girls in high school and
college. He had been sexually involved with three girls—with

ver an extended period of time—and had no real problems performing sexually.

He had been drafted when he dropped out of college at twenty-one, and he spent the next three years in the Army. While in the service he had continued to have sex with both males and females, although he said that he had continued to feel very guilty about such behavior.

He was in the Army when he met Katrina while attending church in a community near the base. She was a delightful person who shared many of his interests, and they had decided to marry after dating for six months. Because of her strong religious convictions, they had decided not to have sexual relations before marriage. Afraid that she would be unable to accept his previous sexual involvement, Ross had felt it better not to bring up the past. Discussing his decision to marry, Ross told the counselor that he had done so because he had always wanted to have a wife and children and lead a normal family life.

Although he had been tempted, Ross had remained faithful to Katrina for the first four years of their marriage. While sex had never been a big thing in their marriage, Ross said that they both seemed to enjoy being close to each other, and on the occasions when this led to sex, it had seemed pleasant enough for both.

Ross said, however, that things had changed when he was taking a night class and met a professor who had shown a special interest in him and asked him to join him for a cup of coffee one evening after class. Although at first he refused the professor's invitation to have sexual relations with him, Ross admitted that he had been strongly attracted to him and had given in several nights later. Ross became very involved, both physically and emotionally, with his teacher and had been startled and perplexed at the end of the quarter when the professor had broken off the relationship, saying that he was not interested in anything permanent. It was shortly after the abrupt termination of this relationship that Ross began to go out actively seeking other males.

Expecting his wife to divorce him on the spot when she learned of his homosexual activities, Ross was puzzled when she expressed a willingness to continue the marriage in spite of being hurt and shocked. When Ross told her in later conversations that she deserved something better and that he had always enjoyed the company of men more than that of women, Katrina continued to insist that they could work things out. Any attempt to discuss the termination of the marriage was pushed aside by Katrina, who continued to frustrate Ross by saying that her love for him was so strong that if she had to, she would be willing to accept his homosexuality and allow him to go out with men when he needed to. Her only request was that he not tell her of his activities.

After several weeks of counseling, Ross said that he was more restless than ever and that he really wanted a divorce so that he could pursue a gay life-style. He could not, however, bring himself to hurt Katrina by asking her outright for a divorce. He expressed the hope that instead she would become so unhappy with his conduct that she would take the initiative in seeking a divorce, thus relieving him of the guilt which he anticipated if he instigated the break-up of the marriage. Despite Ross' lack of sexual attention to her and his continuing sexual involvement with men, Katrina had gone about her daily living as if nothing was wrong.

Discussion

As surprising as it may seem to some, there are homosexuals who choose to marry. Many of them elect not to tell their intended spouses of their sexual feelings. They may evade the issue entirely or even refuse to admit to themselves that they have a sexual problem for a number of reasons. Some have said in counseling sessions that they married because they wanted to have a home and children like other people. Those who find it difficult to accept the possibility that they may be homosexual sometimes enter marriage with the hope that it will eliminate the problem. Still others marry as a cover-up for their homosexual life-styles.

Whatever the reasons for individuals with strong inclinations toward homosexuality marrying heterosexuals, the problem does come up in marriage, probably more than we realize. While it may be possible for some couples to maintain a relationship under such circumstances, the chances seem almost nonexistent if one spouse waits until after marriage to spring such news on his or her partner. In some cases the shock proves to be so great that the heterosexual partner simply walks out and never speaks to his or her spouse again.

We will not go into all the issues surrounding homosexuality, but it does seem unthinkable that individuals who recognize their own homosexual tendencies would attempt to conceal such feelings from someone they hope to live with as husband or wife. Since we do know that in adults strong desires for sexual relationships with someone of the same sex are not easy to change, entering marriage with the knowledge that one does not have sexual feelings and attitudes similar to those of one's spouse is, in our opinion, a serious mistake.

Since we do know, however, that some individuals choose to do just this—to keep their sexual preferences a secret—we must ask how a person might determine whether the individual he or she hopes to marry has homosexual tendencies which could later cause open conflict. While it may be difficult to tell in some cases, the following questions and suggestions can be used in an effort to learn more about one's intended husband or wife and his or her sexual preferences. If there is some reason to suspect that something might be wrong, it would be appropriate to ask:

(1) Is there an absence of any erotic or sexual response to members of the opposite sex? This is, of course, the most obvious clue that something may be wrong. If the person is unable to perform (if sexual intercourse has been attempted), or if he or she is not sexually stimulated by intimate physical contact with a member of the opposite sex, this should raise some questions. While the matter of whether to have sexual intercourse prior to marriage may be a moral issue for many, the absence of the *desire* to do so strongly suggests that sexual problems exist. It should therefore be emphasized that, when a male or female shows an aversion for or lack of sexual interest in his or her

partner, professional help should be considered.

(2) Does the individual seem unreasonably uncomfortable or uninterested in the presence of the opposite sex?

(3) Does the person have a history of shunning dates or contacts with members of the opposite sex?

(4) Does the person shy away from any involvement in activities generally associated with being masculine or feminine?

(5) Is there a history of previous homosexual encounters or gossip to that effect among those who have known the person for some time?

(6) Does your intended spouse claim to be bisexual? Some authorities feel that most individuals who boast that they are bisexual are probably more inclined toward homosexuality than heterosexuality.

(7) Does your date try to convince you that it is sophisticated to go both ways or suggest that you might want to be involved with someone of the same sex sometime in the future?

One of the most obvious ways to determine if one's future spouse has homosexual leanings is to ask. If it seems that the person is being deceitful or evasive regarding sexual feelings, ask direct questions and insist on straight answers. Do not assume, as some couples do, that once you are married nature will take over and all sexual problems will resolve themselves. Since sex is such an important part of marriage, couples thinking of marriage should approach the discussion of sexual matters in as much depth as they would financial, moral, religious, social, physical, or psychological concerns.

It is also possible to gain considerable insight regarding the potential for sexual problems of this sort by observing the relationship between one's boyfriend or girlfriend and his or her parents. For example, an over-protective, possessive, domineering mother who refuses to let her son participate in activities usually enjoyed by other males could be an indication that problems exist. Or the mother who is always telling her daughter that men are no good and cannot be trusted may have set the stage for poor relationships with men, sexually and otherwise. Likewise, the father who is cold, distant, cruel, or overly critical of either a son or a daughter might well have conditioned his children to think negatively about members of the opposite sex.

A word of caution. It should be emphasized that an occasional fantasy about sexual involvement with a person of the same sex does not mean that an individual is homosexual. Most if not all people have had such thoughts at some time. Neither should the person who has had a fleeting homosexual experience be classified as a homosexual. While homosexual fantasies and acts can be indications of sexual problems, caution should be exercised in any decision until there has been a thorough analysis and discussion of such behavior by the individuals involved. If doubts persist, professional expertise should be sought.

marry someone who will not let bygones be bygones

Bea, a twenty-two-year-old secretary, came with tears in her eyes to the mental health clinic to discuss problems with Brian, her twenty-eight-year-old fiancé. Saying that they were to be married in two months, she wanted to know what she could do to help Brian forget her past sexual escapades with another man.

Sobbing softly, Bea then began to tell how, during the six months they had dated, Brian had pestered her to discuss with him her sex life before they had met. Insisting that her previous sexual behavior had no relationship to the way she felt about him, Bea had refused to discuss the matter with Brian for several months. When he had continued to probe and insist that they should have no secrets between them, Bea had weakened and admitted that she had had an affair with an older man when she was nineteen. Refusing to discuss it any further at the time, even when Brian assured her that it would make no difference in the way he felt toward her, Bea had thought the matter closed when Brian went for a week without bringing it up again. However, soon he again began to insist that Bea tell him all the details of her involvement. Though reluctant to do so, Bea had given in after a hike in the woods in which they had seemed especially close; she told him everything. Brian reassured her that he still cared for her and appreciated her openness with him, and Bea once again thought the matter closed, since Brian seemed unconcerned about her previous sexual involvement.

In the weeks that followed, however, Bea reported that Brian gradually began to change in the way he acted toward her. He became sullen and sometimes went for long periods of time without speaking to her. At other times he would speak sharply to her for no apparent reason and on several occasions had pushed her away when she tried to kiss or embrace him.

Troubled by his behavior, Bea had finally confronted Brian with her feelings and insisted that he tell her what was bothering him. Although at first he refused to do so, Brian had eventually admitted that he could not forget that Bea had had sex with another man. Though he had tried in every way he knew, he insisted that he could not erase from his mind the picture of Bea in bed with her lover, even though it had happened long before they met each other or planned to marry. Hoping that discussing it would help, they had spent an entire night talking about nothing else. Feeling somewhat relieved when Brian failed to mention it on their next two dates, Bea tried to change the subject when Brian brought the matter up again three nights later. Her efforts were to no avail, however, as Brian began to demand that she go over the incident again and again, describing in great detail everything that took place.

Not content just to hear Bea's description of the events, Brian began in the weeks that followed to insist that Bea go with him to places where she had been with her former lover. Even on occasions when they had enjoyed dinner with no mention of her affair, Brian would suddenly say, "I guess you are thinking of the time you were in this same restaurant with Sean." Usually, after Bea tried to convince Brian that she had not been thinking of Sean at all, a big fight would ensue, and Bea would end up in tears after Brian called her a slut. This had happened so often that Bea was convinced that Brian went out of his way to take her to places where he knew she had been with Sean just to make her feel guilty or to punish her. At times overwhelmed with guilt, Bea would say, "I would do anything to erase my past and be able to come to Brian as a virgin, something he has told me so often he wanted in a wife."

Though he had refused to come in with Bea, Brian made an appointment to see the counselor alone. While readily admitting that it was wrecking the relationship, Brian confessed that he could not stop thinking about Bea and Sean together. Rather than getting better, he said that he was becoming more and more obsessed with the thought. He had even thought of killing Sean or at least calling him and telling him off for what he had done to Bea. Although he admitted that he had had sexual relationships with other women, he saw this as an entirely different matter. Even though he could agree that women had as much right as men to engage in sex with more than one partner, he had failed miserably in applying such logic to his relationship with Bea.

Though continuing to plan for the wedding, Brian said that he had begun to wonder if he should marry Bea. The thought of breaking up with her, however, was so painful that he had decided to go ahead with the marriage even when he felt so strongly that what she had done was unforgivable. Rather than talking about how Bea's previous sexual relationship made him feel as a man, Brian continued to insist that he was not troubled by the sex in itself but more by the fact that Bea had let a man take advantage of her and use her without any concern for her well-being.

When the counselor asked Brian to return for joint sessions with Bea to discuss their relationship further, Brian refused to do so but did agree to return for an individual session. However, he failed to keep his appointment. In her next session, Bea stated that Brian had said that their sexual problems were personal and should not be discussed with anyone else. He had even insisted that Bea not see the counselor again. When she expressed a desire to return, they agreed that she would go for only two more sessions.

In the remaining sessions, Bea continued to focus on ways in which she could help Brian with his problem. When the counselor tried to convince her that she could do little to help Brian with his problem unless he expressed a willingness to work together on it, Bea continued to insist that there must be something she could do. Finally, convinced that the advice she hoped for was not forthcoming, Bea asked, "Well, how can I learn to live with the problem? I love Brian with all my heart and plan to go ahead with the marriage despite the hurt and pain he inflicts on me. Even if I knew for certain that Brian would throw my past sexual behavior up to me every day for the rest of my life, I would never consider calling the wedding off, because I know I could never love another man the way I love him."

Discussion

A better title for this case might be "The Husband Who Neither Forgives nor Forgets." About the only thing which can be said with certainty about this relationship is that both parties are going into the marriage with some awareness of the problems which they can anticipate as a result of Brian's obsession with Bea's previous sexual relationship. The interaction between this couple raises many questions regarding their potential for a successful and healthy marriage.

Many individuals would become upset when confronted for the first time with the revelation that the person they planned to marry had engaged in some activity which they view as immoral or distasteful. Some couples would call off the engagement altogether. Others might go through a period of grieving, with a gradual acceptance and adjustment to the situation. Brian, however, seems unable to do either. He refuses to let go of the relationship while appearing to be unable to accept the events which have occurred. In fact, Brian's feelings seem to be growing more and more intense. His inability to handle the situation despite a reasonable passage of time and Bea's insistence that she has changed and loves only him suggests that more is involved than just Brian's feelings about Bea's sexual conduct. His desire to hurt Bea again and again with constant reminders of her past behavior is significant and should not be brushed aside by anyone anticipating marriage to such a person.

Perhaps even more significant is the degree of self-punitiveness involved. Brian goes to great lengths to hurt himself, as evidenced by his return visits to places which will remind him afresh of Bea's involvement with another man. Such behavior might be compared to picking at a sore, refusing to let it heal.

Of equal concern in this case is Bea's willingness to continue subjecting herself to such torture. Although she insists that Brian's behavior toward her is painful to endure, she continues to go back again and again, as if asking to be hurt. Apparently unable to accept the fact that Brian's attitude is indicative of some rather deep-seated emotional problems, Bea seems determined to blame herself for his condition and feels compelled to find a solution. Such thinking suggests that Bea is not very realistic in her expectations of their relationship together. She seems to believe that once they are married the problem will take care of itself. Of even greater concern is her decision to go ahead with the marriage even though she may be persecuted and maligned for the rest of her life.

While people can change, it will be emphasized more than once in this book that persons should never enter marriage unless they can accept the prospective spouse as he or she is prior to marriage. Entering marriage with the idea that one's spouse will make major personality changes is a risky thing at best. More often than not, long-standing patterns of behavior are adhered to even more firmly after marriage. If Bea insists on going ahead with the marriage, she might well expect to be reminded for the rest of her life of her "unpardonable sin." While there are marriages which manage to endure even though one spouse seems to delight in inflicting punishment—either physical or verbal—while the other seems perfectly willing to exist as a martyr, such relationships are unhealthy, to say the least. The spouse who persists in abusing or degrading his or her partner is no less healthy than the spouse who continues to permit the abuse. Such a relationship is destructive not only for the couple; the potential for harm to children who may be born into such an environment is frightening.

In summary, caution should be exercised in becoming involved in a serious relationship with a person who is unable to forget or accept past behavior, even when the act may have been reprehensible in the accuser's eyes. The continued flagellation of self or others, even when the behavior engaged in is unacceptable, serves no real purpose other than to inflict pain on all concerned. Marriage to a person with such tendencies can result in a lifetime of being constantly reminded of one's failures and misdeeds. Such attacks over a prolonged period of time will eventually affect most individuals and inevitably lead to resentment, low self-esteem, and feelings of worthlessness and sinfulness.

In evaluating the potential for the development of such a relationship, it would be important to raise the sorts of questions listed below.

Does my boyfriend or girlfriend:
(1) respect me?
(2) seem able to accept me for what I am now rather than judging me on the basis of past behavior?
(3) seem unable to trust me in situations similar to those in which I have made mistakes in the past?
(4) seem unable to forgive?
(5) keep bringing up things from the past to hurt me or himself/herself?
(6) seem to enjoy bringing up such reminders?
(7) act as if I should pay for my mistakes forever?

Am I:
(1) able to accept and respect myself?
(2) able to forgive myself for past mistakes?
(3) encouraging or permitting a continuation of behavior which is harmful to both of us?
(4) guilty and deserving of everlasting punishment for my sins or wrongdoings?

marry someone who
runs away from problems

Mindy and Clint agreed in their opening counseling session that they were tired of all the turmoil in their marriage and were considering divorce. Neither wanted to be the one to initiate divorce proceedings, however. Sitting quietly during the session while Mindy did most of the talking, Clint asked to see the counselor alone the following week.

Alone with the counselor, Clint said that he really wanted the divorce but wanted Mindy to leave him. Admitting that he had always had difficulty making decisions about anything, Clint said that marriage had been Mindy's idea all along and that consequently it should be her responsibility to make the decision to end it. When questioned by the counselor as to his role in the decision to marry, Clint replied that he had let himself be roped into marriage. Describing himself as always having had trouble saying no to people, Clint gave his view of how Mindy had manipulated him into marrying her.

When she had first broached the subject of marriage, he had immediately balked. Not one to give up easily, Mindy then began to lecture Clint on the way he had taken advantage of her sexually. Admitting that Mindy had been a virgin when he first went to bed with her, Clint said that she had been the one who had pushed to have sexual relations. When he had continued to refuse to marry her after several weeks of persuasive maneuvers on her part, Mindy had accused him outright of using her for sex. After she had continued this line of attack for several weeks, saying that no man would want her now, Clint had reluctantly given in and agreed to marriage.

After the marriage things had gotten worse, and Clint confessed that he was still unable to stand up to Mindy. Describing her as a very volatile and aggressive person, he said that he had come to the conclusion that the best way to deal with Mindy was to avoid her when possible. If this was impossible, he would say very little in response to her criticisms or attacks on him. Saying that he hated arguing and violence, he would either leave the house or just tune his wife out when she began one of her tirades.

In the next joint session, Clint again sat quietly while Mindy did most of the talking. When she would try to force him to participate by asking him direct questions, Clint would smile and nod his head or speak in monosyllables. Occasionally he would reply to one of his wife's questions with the response "If you say so."

Obviously perturbed by Clint's passive approach to anything she said, Mindy told the counselor that this was typical of their exchanges with each other. Admitting that Clint seldom criticized her or expressed dissatisfaction about anything, Mindy said, "I know there are times when he must feel very unhappy or angry. If I say something that hurts his feelings, he will usually withdraw and pout for days. I have a hot temper and get mad easily, but I am soon over it and everything is forgotten. But Clint usually prefers to ignore things until I explode."

When Clint continued to remain silent, Mindy began discussing the many things he did which she found irritating. She described herself as a very punctual person and said that Clint's tardiness drove her up the wall. He would, for example, often show up late for dinner and had the previous week shown up late for a dinner party she was giving with the excuse that it had slipped his mind. On other occasions he would fail to show up at all when they had something planned. He would frequently bring home unannounced guests for dinner. His failure to subtract checks which he had written in the checkbook not only made her angry but had proved embarrassing on a number of occasions when their account had been overdrawn. Just that week the manager of the supermarket where Mindy shopped weekly had called to inform her that a check had been returned for insufficient funds. An immaculate housekeeper, she had fought with Clint many times over the way he left his dirty clothes strewn all over the house. Even when she had put additional clothes hampers at strategic places throughout the house, he still threw his clothes on the floor, sometimes within two feet of a hamper.

In sexual matters Mindy said sarcastically that she must have a much stronger sex drive than Clint, since she usually had to take the initiative if they had sexual relations. Although both Clint and Mindy said they found the other physically attractive, Mindy said she sometimes felt very unattractive. Clint interrupted to explain that Mindy was especially hurt when they tried to have sex and he was unable to perform. Mindy said, "It does hurt when you are unable to arouse your own husband." When she would attempt to discuss with Clint her frustration in regard to their sexual problems, he would typically say it was nothing to get upset about and turn over as if to sleep. Not satisfied to let it drop, Mindy would insist on talking about it until an argument developed. On more than one occasion when Mindy had been talking about their sexual difficulties or some other problem between them, she had discovered that Clint had fallen asleep.

Discussion

One of the most serious obstacles in the establishment of a good marital relationship is a partner who will not deal with problems openly when difficulties arise.

It is obvious even to a casual observer that Mindy is very resentful. Not so obvious is the fact that Clint is also a very resentful and angry person. He seems unable to deal with his feelings in a direct way, however. Consequently he has developed a way of getting back at Mindy, which is very destructive for the marriage. Rather than confronting Mindy directly when he is displeased, he does things which would irritate or infuriate most people. Although he might appear to be a calm and even-tempered person, his seemingly more passive and non-violent ways of expressing dissatisfaction mask some very intense feelings of resentment and hostility. Such tactics are usually more destructive in the long run than are Mindy's explosive outbursts of anger and hostility.

Mindy admits that she has a hot temper and ventilates anger very freely and with little provocation. Once she has done this, however, the incident is soon forgotten and she is ready to go on about the business of living. Not so with Clint. Refusing even to admit that he is angry or that a problem exists, he allows his anger to smolder or pouts and goes for days without speaking.

Such people often appear to others and to themselves as long-suffering and slow to anger, the type who will bear all sorts of injustices rather than rock the boat. In truth they are usually neither kind nor slow to anger. They are instead often overly sensitive to anything they perceive as being critical. They become hurt and angry very easily. Rather than dealing with their frustrations and hostilities in a direct way, however, they resort to more subtle ways. Though subtle and indirect, they can be very vicious and cruel in their retaliation. They know full well that one of the most effective ways to punish a spouse or to get revenge is to pout or to ignore the other person. Some go for long periods refusing to discuss the issue, even if their spouse begs and pleads for forgiveness.

Rather than being tolerant and compassionate, such individuals are really often very aggressive people who have chosen passivity as a way of expressing hostility or coping with problems which arise in their marriage.

The ways in which such people choose to deal with problems in their relationships with others are endless. They may, for example, fail to respond to sexual overtures from their spouses or even become impotent or frigid when they do attempt sexual relations. This can, of course, prove to be devastating to the husband or wife, who tends to assume the blame. Or they may, as Clint did, engage in many practices which they know their mates find irritating or intolerable, all the time feigning innocence. With Clint this included forgetting appointments, bringing guests home unannounced for dinner, throwing his clothes on the floor, falling asleep in the middle of conversations, bouncing checks, and just walking away from his wife when the situation seemed to call for conversation or confrontation. Some people escape by drinking or working all the time.

No matter how the anger or unhappiness is demonstrated, the intent is usually that of hurting the other person or escaping from a situation perceived as stressful. Although they may appear to be willing to go to great lengths to maintain peace, such people are often masters at evading problems or confrontations. They are often skilful at inflicting pain or putting the other person down passively. Rather than solving the problem, their behavior only intensifies or makes the problem worse.

While we have focused on Clint and his ways of avoiding any direct confrontation whenever conflict arises, the problem can exist in many forms and for many reasons.

Whatever the cause, serious problems do not usually go away just because they are ignored. While hiding their heads in the sand may provide a false sense of security for ostriches, escapism can lead to disaster in marriage. This is not to say that Mindy's way of coping with conflict is always the best and Clint's always wrong. There are times when it is best to walk away when conflict arises. Ventilating anger just for the sake of demonstrating it may in many cases prove to be destructive. What is important if the marriage is to survive is that the couple find ways of dealing with problems in an open and honest way which is acceptable to both.

It cannot be emphasized too often or too strongly that it is just as important to learn how to fight in marriage as it is to learn how to love. Since conflict is inevitable in all marriages, constructive ways of resolving differences must be agreed on if the relationship is to endure. The ways in which individuals settle differences while dating may say more about their chances for success in marriage than anything else.

When problems similar to those experienced by Mindy and Clint are present prior to marriage, serious difficulties can be anticipated after marriage, when two people find themselves spending even more time together in intimate situations in which stress is inevitable.

marry someone with a drug problem

Len opened the marriage counseling session with the statement that he and his wife, Vi, were considering divorce. When asked to elaborate, Len said that they saw life very differently and had almost no interests or values in common.

After listening for about five minutes to Len's elaboration in their lack of mutual interests, Vi interrupted to say that she disagreed with him when he said they had no interests in common. She insisted instead that they really had many things in common, but that Len never asked her to do any of those things with him. Vi then accused Len of preferring to go off with the guys rather than spend time with her.

When Len started to agree that Vi was basically correct in her interpretation, Vi again interrupted to say that their problem in a nutshell was Len's drinking. Asked to elaborate, Vi said that her strong opposition to Len's drinking was at the heart of his statement that they had no common interests. She continued, "We really enjoy a lot of the same things but never get around to doing them together because Len wants to go out drinking every night. He seldom asks me to go anymore, and when he does I usually refuse, since I know he will get loaded before the night is over."

Admitting that he liked to drink, Len countered that he felt it was unfair for Vi to ask him to stop. She had known that he liked to drink before they married, and he had made no promises that he would stop drinking afterwards. When Vi started to object, Len announced that he had neither the desire nor intention of giving up alcohol.

After regaining the floor, Vi admitted that she had been aware of Len's drinking prior to their marriage and also acknowledged that Len had made it clear that he planned to continue his drinking. Vi said, however, that she had believed that after marriage she could convince Len to give up alcohol or at least cut down on his intake. He had instead begun to drink even more heavily. He had now reached the point where three or four drinks each night was, in his thinking, a light night of drinking. When asked by the counselor if he thought he had a drinking problem, Len replied, "No, I drink a good bit but I can quit any time I want to. I can go several weeks without a drink and it doesn't bother me. I feel that I have cut down on my drinking. Because Vi gets so upset, I agreed to drink only on weekends." At this point Vi again interrupted to say, "Yes, but you still drink a six-pack of beer every night of the week." Turning to the counselor, Vi said, "If Len switches to beer or wine he does not consider it drinking. But he gets just as high and can't seem to get through one evening without a few beers. He will look for any excuse to drink. If friends drop in, the first thing he will do is offer them a drink. While they have one drink, Len may have two or three."

In an attempt to defend himself, Len argued that in the town where they lived there was nothing else to do but drink. Since they had lived there only a short time, he knew very few people. Because of his job as a construction worker, they moved frequently. Len said that his nightly visits to bars enabled him to relax and meet people he would otherwise never meet due to their restricted social life. He insisted that he went to bars as much to talk and be with people as to drink.

Again attacking Vi for her lack of interest in the sorts of things he enjoyed, Len said that if they had more fun together he would not feel so compelled to go out each night.

Referring to their sex life, both Vi and Len agreed that it was miserable. When Len accused Vi of never enjoying sex or making any attempt to be sexually attractive, Vi retorted that the only time he paid her any attention was when he had been drinking. "I have told him how I hate the smell of liquor on his breath when he tries to kiss me and how it turns me off. But he doesn't pay any attention to me. Even when I give in and go ahead and have sex, most of the time he is so drunk that he is impotent. If he would just cut out his drinking, we could have a good marriage." Obviously angered by Vi's statement, Len shouted, "I like being married to you, but unless you get off my back about my drinking, I'm ready to call it quits. While I hate the thought of being alone, I would prefer that to your constant nagging."

Discussion

The use of alcohol and other drugs can have a profound effect on a marriage. The potential spouse who appears to have a drinking problem in all likelihood is going to have that problem after marriage. Again it should be emphasized that marriage is not apt to change a person. Undesirable traits or habits only tend to become more firmly entrenched after marriage.

The last person to recognize or admit to having a drinking problem is usually the problem drinker. He or she will go to great lengths to deny that a problem exists or to cover it up if it can no longer be ignored. Many will turn to beer or wine under the false impression that one is not an alcoholic so long as he or she sticks to these beverages, when in truth it makes little difference where the alcohol comes from.

As strange as it may sound, individuals like Vi often seem attracted to persons with a drinking or other drug problem, despite their insistence that they find such habits deplorable. Everyone is acquainted with the women who stays married to an alcoholic husband for twenty or thirty years, apparently getting very little that seems to be rewarding or positive for herself. She may spend a major portion of her time taking care of her husband and fussing and pleading with him to quit his drinking. She may look for hidden bottles and pour the contents down the sink when she finds them. She may even leave him but usually comes back after a few days, and the pattern is repeated again and again. With these couples it is hard to determine who has the bigger problem.

While we tend to think of the problem drinker in terms of a skid-row bum or town drunk, the problem permeates our society, from people in the highest levels of business and government to those trapped in the poverty of the most wretched ghetto. For many years viewed as primarily a problem for males, the use of alcohol and drugs is now a serious problem for females as well.

Unfortunately, the problem for both men and women is increasing rather than decreasing. While there are those who take comfort in the decline of the popularity of certain drugs, viewing a return to the use of alcohol as an improvement, we cannot escape the fact that the abuse of alcohol is still the most serious drug problem in this country today.

While the abuse of alcohol and other drugs is a national disaster, the potential for disruption and conflict in marriage is one of major proportions. Not only is the abuser a source of trouble for himself or herself, the damage to his or her spouse and children can be profound.

If drugs can play such a major role in the break-up of homes and marriages, how does one identify, prior to marriage, the man or woman who has such tendencies? The fact is that there are no easy ways to detect the problem drinker or drug abuser. The person who suffers from DT's or who is constantly stoned out of his mind can usually be identified and labeled accordingly. If people want to badly enough, however, they can usually deceive the person they plan to marry. They may not even know themselves that they have a problem. Even when it is obvious that a serious problem exists, the other partner may be blinded by "love" and choose to ignore the warning signals or convince himself or herself that things will change after marriage.

Despite the difficulty in making such a judgment, there are certain clues which can help to spot the potential problem drinker or drug abuser. If you suspect that your girlfriend or boyfriend might have a drinking or drug problem, you might want to ask the following questions. (While the word alcohol is most often used below, the questions are just as applicable for any other drug.)

Does he or she:
   (1) have to have a drink to relax, carry on a conversation, or relate to others in a social situation?
   (2) drink whenever problems come up?
   (3) plan ahead to make sure that alcohol is always available?
   (4) become irritable if drinks are not available?
   (5) have to have several drinks or beers each night?

(6) get drunk often?

(7) get angry or refuse to discuss it whenever it is suggested that he or she might have a drinking problem?

(8) insist that he or she has no problem or can quit at any time?

(9) insist that you cannot become an alcoholic as long as you drink only beer or wine?

(10) keep insisting that you drink also?

(11) lose time from work or school as a result of drinking?

(12) have problems functioning in other areas of life due to drinking (i.e., playing, sex, social relationships, family)?

(13) seem unable to stop drinking until drunk once the first drink has been consumed?

(14) drink one drink after another quickly?

(15) suffer from loss of memory or blackouts while drinking?

(16) become abusive or overly aggressive while drinking?

(17) promise to quit drinking after marriage?

(18) promise before marriage to quit but fail to do so?

(19) drive while drinking or engage in other activities with little concern for personal safety or the safety of others?

(20) show little or no effect after consuming a large quantity of alcohol?

(21) spend a lot of time drinking alone?

While the use of any drug is for many a moral issue, it is not our purpose to become involved in such issues. Neither do we wish to give the impression that anyone who drinks or uses drugs moderately is necessarily a bad marriage risk. Many experts on alcohol and drugs agree, however, that problems can be anticipated if the person:

(1) deliberately sets out to get drunk frequently.

(2) uses drugs or alcohol as an escape whenever problems or stressful situations arise.

(3) is usually unhappy or despondent unless high on drugs or alcohol.

(4) depends on the bottle for courage to face life.

While we have focused on alcohol or drugs obtained without a doctor's prescription, it should be emphasized that many people have serious drug problems unknowingly sanctioned by their physicians, who prescribe tranquilizers or other drugs indiscriminately.

While the use of alcohol or other drugs can in itself constitute a major problem for couples, it can also cover up more basic personality problems, defects, and interpersonal conflicts which may exist in the relationship.

marry someone with "savior syndrome"

Jon and Meg asked to see someone for counseling in February prior to their proposed marriage in June.

Jon was a twenty-seven-year-old minister who was scheduled to complete his theological training in May. He said that he was eager to graduate, since his greatest desire in life was to help others. He revealed that for this reason he had first considered being a physician but had changed his major in college when his grades in science had not turned out as well as he had expected. Although he had at first been disappointed to leave the study of medicine, he felt that he had ample opportunities to be of service to others in the ministry.

Meg, two years older than Jon, had been married but had been divorced for two years. Although still an attractive woman, Meg gave the impression that she had not paid much attention to her health or physical appearance in recent months. Unemployed at the time of the first session, Meg said that she had been employed in a series of jobs since her divorce but had found nothing she really liked. She replied heavily on alimony payments for support and showed little interest in preparing herself for a career or a better job.

Jon had scheduled the appointment for counseling because he was concerned about Meg's drinking, smoking, and general neglect of herself. Though Meg was only twenty-nine, her doctor had informed her that she was already showing symptoms of emphysema and urged her to quit smoking. She smoked two packs of cigarettes a day and drank at least a fifth of liquor each week, but Meg had promised both Jon and her doctor that she was going to quit drinking and cut down on her smoking. She had, however, failed to do either, but continued to say that if Jon would just be patient and help her, she would eventually lick the problems.

61479

Jon had repeatedly threatened to end the relationship when Meg failed to show any evidence of change. On a number of occasions he had walked out. He always returned, however, with the explanation that he just could not turn his back on Meg at a time when she needed him so much.

When he would return, usually after staying away two or three days, he would find Meg in her apartment in a drunken, helpless state. Even when she was sober, Meg seldom cleaned her apartment, and Jon said that empty whiskey bottles and beer cans were simply thrown in a corner of the room where they remained until he cleared them out in one of his periodic clean-up campaigns. Unless he forced her to go out to a restaurant with him or prepared a meal for her in his apartment, she almost never ate. On several occasions he had had nearby restaurants send lunch over to Meg in his absence. He would usually find the food untouched when he returned.

Jon also said that he had been hurt by Meg's involvement with other men. On three different occasions he had been to the apartment and found Meg in bed with another man. Although she admitted that she did occasionally sleep with other men, Meg reminded Jon again and again during the session that he was the man she loved and wanted to marry. Jon responded by saying that Meg had made similar statements in the past, but this had not kept her from going out with other men. When this happened they would usually have a bitter confrontation followed by a long discussion, prayer, begging for forgiveness, and promises to do better in the future.

In the second session Jon began to discuss Meg's lack of responsibility in financial areas. This was prompted by the events of the night before, when he had gone to her apartment and found her in tears with a man from a collection agency who was threatening to take legal action unless she paid a long overdue bill at a local department store. The man had been placated when Jon had written him a check and promised to pay the rest later. In discussing the matter further, Jon revealed that this was not an isolated occurrence. Meg had often run up bills which she made no attempt to pay. The month before he had helped her raise the money to keep her car from being repossessed. When confronted with her failure to meet her financial obligations, Meg responded that she was not a dishonest person but just did not know how to handle money wisely.

Jon came in for the third session alone after several of his seminary friends had told him in no uncertain terms that he was a fool to go through with his plans to marry Meg. He resented their interference and had accused them of lacking compassion. He said that to turn away from anyone in need was un-Christian, but to do so with someone you really loved was unforgivable. With both his friends and the marriage counselor, Jon had gone into a long discussion of Meg's tragic childhood: the death of her father when she was eleven, her alcoholic mother, and her several moves from one family of relatives to another.

With a considerable show of emotion regarding Meg's poor family situation, Jon reiterated his intention of seeing to it that Meg received the love she had never been shown as a child or in her first marriage. If he succeeded in doing so, he believed that Meg would eventually respond and turn out to be the kind of wife he could be proud of.

Discussion

Even the most casual readers of the above case would probably be concerned about Meg's mental status, and they should be. She is obviously a very distressed young woman. But there is reason to be concerned about Jon as well. Both Meg and Jon are exceedingly needy people. One has a strong need to take care of, while the other has a strong need to be taken care of.

Though it is important to be compassionate and concerned with helping others, it is equally important that human beings realize that there are some people who cannot or will not be helped. Individuals who ignore this basic psychological truth are sometimes referred to as having a savior syndrome or complex. Women who marry men with a serious drinking problem hoping to reform them after marriage often fall into this category. Men may marry prostitutes or other women they view as immoral for a similar reason. Many women are accused of wanting to mother their boyfriends or husbands, whom they see as incapable of taking care of themselves. Men frequently feel the need to step in and prevent a helpless young woman from throwing her life away or save her from unscrupulous persons. Both men and women have married known homosexuals with the intention of reforming them or saving them from themselves.

It cannot be emphasized too strongly that helping others is an admirable quality. However, marriage counselors are all too familiar with the frequency with which individuals with an overwhelming need to feel needed and to help others get involved with persons who have an overwhelming need to be taken care of or mothered. Despite their denials, there are reformers who are unhappy if their goals are achieved. Likewise, there are many people who, having married persons suffering from some serious physical or emotional handicap, would be frustrated if their spouses suddenly changed and became more capable and self-sufficient persons. They might resent this, for it could mean that they would no longer feel needed.

While some couples like Meg and Jon stay married, most people would not consider such a relationship to be a healthy one. Although Meg is obviously in need of help, it is quite likely that the relationship between Jon and Meg will be mutually destructive in the long run.

marry someone who is extremely jealous and possessive

Renee and Chris first came for marriage counseling after they had been separated for two weeks. After nine years of marriage, Renee said, she had reached the conclusion that she had to get away from Chris for a few weeks in order to figure out whether or not she wanted to stay married to him. Although Chris had been strongly opposed to the separation, he had finally given in with great reluctance to Renee's demand for it.

In talking with the marriage counselor, however, Renee said they had not really been separated, since Chris called her several times each day telling her how much he needed her and begging her to return home. On several occasions he had dropped by the office where she worked and asked to have lunch with her. Although she had resented the intrusion, Renee said that she could not stand the hurt look in her husband's eyes when she asked him to leave. Consequently, he usually ended up coming along. When she begged him not to call or stop by, he accused her of wanting to be with other men instead of with him. Even though she attempted to convince him that she had no interest in seeing any other man, Chris continued to accuse her of wanting to separate for this reason.

In subsequent sessions Renee complained that even before their marriage Chris had been very jealous and protective. At parties or on other social occasions she was never allowed to dance or talk with other men without Chris' interrupting or breaking in. If a strange man even held the door open for her or helped her with an armload of groceries, Chris would become resentful and sullen. Even an occasional trip to the movies or to play bridge with other women aroused his ire. Although he admitted that Renee could not possibly be involved with other men on such occasions, he still insisted that arrangements be made with other couples so that he might be included. When questioned by the counselor as to why he felt this way, Chris remained adamant in his contention that couples in love should do everything together. If they chose not to, Chris interpreted this as proof that they no longer cared for each other. Even insisting on going shopping with his wife, he defended his actions by saying that it was not safe for a woman to be alone on the streets, even during the day.

Although he freely admitted that he was guilty of such practices, Chris maintained throughout the sessions that he saw nothing wrong with his behavior and only did these things because he loved his wife so much. Again insisting that husbands and wives should do everything together and have no secrets from each other, he said he felt that Renee's desire for privacy or for a few moments alone was an indication that she no longer loved him.

His insistence on having his wife with him at all times had resulted in fewer and fewer invitations over the years, even from his male friends. Although they were fond of Renee, they had felt it inappropriate when Chris insisted on taking her on fishing trips or to play golf. If they expressed to Chris their dissatisfaction with such an arrangement, he would refuse to accept the invitation. When Renee finally put her foot down and informed Chris that she did not like golf or fishing and refused to go with him, he had given up these activities himself and insisted that they find other things which they enjoyed doing together.

Renee admitted that she had been insecure in the first years of her marriage and liked Chris' attention and his determination to protect and care for her. With the passage of time, however, she had grown to find such behavior irritating and confessed that she felt that she was being stifled in her growth as a person. At times she felt as if she was being smothered by her husband's constant attention and surveillance.

When she tried to tell Chris that she needed some time alone, he would respond by saying that he was miserable without her. Even Renee's request that she be permitted to take a few days alone to visit her parents in another city was totally unacceptable to Chris. In the nine years they had been married, they had never spent a night apart. Convinced that they had great times when they were together, Chris said that he found it impossible to believe that Renee did not share his pleasure in being together all the time. Stating very emphatically that his wife met all his needs, Chris insisted that he had no need or desire to do anything with anyone else, male or female.

When Chris promised to give Renee more freedom and time to herself if she would return home, she reluctantly agreed to give it another chance. With the counselor's help, certain ground rules were agreed on to permit both Chris and Renee to spend more time each week involved in separate activities. Chris repeatedly violated the agreement, however, saying that he found it impossible to live in the same house with Renee and not be concerned and involved in her comings and goings.

When he continued to violate the contract despite Renee's repeated warnings that she would not tolerate his doing so, she packed her belongings and moved to an apartment. This also failed because of Chris' nightly visits and phone calls. He finally gave Renee an ultimatum: return home or he would file for divorce. At this point Renee contacted an attorney and filed for divorce herself.

Discussion

Possessiveness is often confused with love. There are, however, many differences. Love encourages individual growth and independence. Possessiveness, on the other hand, stifles growth and fosters dependence. To the possessive spouse, the partner is just another object to be owned and controlled as if he or she were no more than an automobile or a valuable piece of art.

While there is usually some element of jealousy in most love relationships between men and women—most people have a tendency to "stake out their claim"—in the case of Chris and Renee the jealousy is obviously excessive. No two people are ever so compatible that they will *always* share the same needs or interests or want to be together all the time. While there is a place for unity and togetherness in marriage, it is also important that both husband and wife recognize that separateness and individuality are also essential if the marriage is to grow and remain healthy.

Although Chris behaved as he did under the guise of love, his actions were more probably the result of his own insecure feelings about the relationship. His attitude was certainly not complimentary to Renee, since it showed a lack of trust in her as a wife and as a woman capable of doing things for herself. Such an attitude is not only demeaning but is a basic cause of low self-esteem and a lack of confidence in oneself as a worthwhile and responsible human being. Like Renee, who admitted that in the earlier stages of their relationship she was very insecure herself, many people find themselves attracted to a partner who showers them with attention and promises of being taken care of. For many of these same people, however, the over-protectiveness and constant togetherness becomes too much.

The only possible way for such a marriage to survive is for the two persons involved to remain locked into a dependency relationship in which one partner dominates almost completely. Such a relationship, as demonstrated by Chris and Renee, is much more characteristic of the symbiotic relationship which exists between infants and parents than of a more mature and satisfying relationship between adults. Individuals who permit themselves to become involved in such a marriage should be prepared for a relationship characterized by many restrictions and a lack of freedom to grow as individuals and as a couple. Of all the complaints expressed by couples experiencing marital problems, it would probably be safe to say that more people complain about a loss of personal identity and the freedom to grow as individuals than anything else. While there are some marriages which manage to endure, even flourish, under circumstances such as those described by Chris and Renee, most people would eventually find such an arrangement intolerable. The prospects for a successful marriage are not promising under the conditions imposed on Renee by Chris. While counseling can often help to bring about positive changes and growth in people like Renee, it is much more difficult for people like Chris. If growth does occur, it can often result in the dissolution of the marriage for the simple reason that the needs which brought the couple together are no longer so prevalent once change occurs.

marry someone who has to be the boss all the time

Audrey, a twenty-four-year-old school teacher, and Neil, a twenty-six-year-old coach, had been married for two years when they decided to see a marriage counselor before seeing a lawyer. Things had gotten so bad between them that Audrey had made an appointment the week before to discuss divorce. She had cancelled the appointment, however, after they had decided to give counseling a try before dissolving the marriage.

Audrey began by saying that she was fed up with the constant fighting which had been going on between them ever since they had married. Neil interrupted to say that they had argued most of the time even while dating. Since they only saw each other occasionally when he came home from college, however, they had failed to realize how serious their problem really was and what it would be like after they were married and had to be together much of the time. Audrey added that they had been so attracted to each other physically and romantically that they had just ignored the warning signs that trouble was inevitable because of their divergent positions on who should be the boss in a marriage.

While things had been stormy the first year, they had gotten much worse the second year after the baby was born. Both agreed that had it not been for their three-month-old child, they would have called it quits months before. Audrey added that even this was no longer enough and voiced the fear that the baby was being adversely affected by the ever-present tension in the home.

In discussing their differences, Audrey and Neil expressed the opinion that the root of their problem was the fear of being dominated. Elaborating further, Audrey said that whenever an issue over which they disagreed came up, they would argue until Neil would explode and eventually insist that the man was the head of the house and say "You as a woman will do what I tell you to do." Audrey would usually retaliate by refusing to do what Neil had asked her to do. Her pat reply was, "No man is going to tell me what to do."

During the initial session, Neil argued that he had no desire to dominate his wife. He said, however, that Audrey resented his asking her to do anything around the house and saw any request as an attempt to boss her around. Even if he planned a surprise outing or dinner in a nice restaurant without first consulting Audrey, she would become furious. Thinking he had been doing something nice for her, Neil found it impossible to understand how Audrey could interpret his behavior as an attempt to run her life.

Confessing that she often felt this way, Audrey accused Neil of behaving in a similar fashion. Even if she asked him to bring in the milk or turn on the television for her, he would usually respond by telling her to do it herself or accuse her of treating him like a small child—always telling him what to do.

Once an argument started, Audrey said, neither would listen to what the other said. Instead, the air would be filled with charges and countercharges until usually the situation got completely out of hand and both became irrational, saying things which neither really felt.

Both Audrey and Neil agreed that most of their fights were over small things and usually centered around the belief that one partner was trying to tell the other what to do. Despite their being at one another's throats much of the time, Neil expressed the belief that beneath all the anger and hostility they still really loved each other. Admitting that she did love Neil and did not want a divorce, Audrey said that they could not continue to live in a state of constant war or competition with each other, as they had for the past two years.

When the counselor reflected during the session that neither seemed to really listen to the other and often interrupted or challenged what the other was saying, Neil responded that this was pretty much the way they acted all the time and that he was not optimistic that they would ever be able to resolve their differences.

Discussion

Some couples seem to thrive on competition. While some competition between husband and wife may be stimulating, with Audrey and Neil it seems to have deteriorated into an all-out war. Their constant battle to dominate the relationship seems to have overshadowed all else. While they admit that they still love and are attracted to each other, their struggle for power has relegated the positive feelings they have for each other to a position of unimportance. They have reached the point where even a polite request to pass the butter is misconstrued as an attempt to tell the other person what to do and to prove who is boss. The determination of each not to be dominated by the other not only destroys any chance they have for a good relationship; it is also negatively affecting the life of their child.

A desire for power is not altogether bad. Most if not all human beings possess the need in varying degrees. Some psychologists and philosophers insist that the need for power is one of our most compelling drives. As with all human urges or drives, however, balance and appropriateness are important. Individuals with overwhelming or exaggerated needs to control others are just as unhealthy as are those with insatiable needs for food, sex, money, or attention. The strong need to dominate and exercise power over others is usually indicative of personal problems which should not be ignored in the selection of a marriage partner. Caution should be exercised if the individual:

(1) always has to be boss.
(2) insists on making all the decisions all the time.
(3) never listens to advice from others.
(4) always disagrees when suggestions are made.
(5) is always contradicting what others say.
(6) seems to have an overwhelming need to dominate and control others.
(7) refuses to respond to requests from others.
(8) has the attitude that others are always trying to manipulate or control him or her.
(9) is overly competitive or aggressive.

(10) always gets angry when losing at sports, games, or other activities.
(11) has the attitude that winning is everything.
(12) is insensitive to other people, willing to do anything to win.

We do not wish to become involved in any controversy over who should be the head of the household. We do, however, want to emphasize that individuals who are planning to marry should come to some consensus on this issue, which is to many people a most critical and sensitive one.

marry someone with a history
of severe emotional problems

Woody, a thirty-eight-year-old commercial pilot, and his thirty-two-year-old wife, Sonya, saw the counselor together on a Wednesday following Sonya's discharge from a local hospital the previous weekend.

Hospital records showed that Sonya had been forcibly brought to the emergency room after taking a number of sleeping pills. Although she had informed her husband that she had taken the pills, Sonya had resisted his efforts to get her to the hospital, insisting that she wanted to be left alone to die. Hospital records also revealed that Sonya had been seen in the emergency room on several other occasions when her husband had been unable to control her following some of their many arguments.

On such occasions Sonya was usually brought in screaming, crying, and abusive to hospital personnel as well as to her husband. On two occasions she had had to be held down while a sedative was administered.

On her most recent admission, the nurses reported that she had spent much of the time in bed curled up in a fetal position with her head under the covers. At these times she would refuse to talk and would turn her head to the wall if anyone entered the room or tried to engage her in conversation. When the doctor entered the room, however, she would clutch his arm tightly, refusing to let go and begging him not to let anyone hurt her anymore. Pleading with him to help her, she spoke in a mixture of baby-talk and incoherent babbling. At other times during her stay she would, for no apparent reason, perk up and talk very openly and intelligently with anyone in the room.

In talking with Woody and Sonya together, the counselor discovered that they had been experiencing marital difficulties for some time. Sonya's major complaint was that her husband just could not understand her and in her opinion made little effort to do so. Since Woody was gone much of the time because of his work as a pilot with a major airline, Sonya reported that she spent a good deal of time alone. She complained of being depressed often and had great difficulty sleeping. She was especially fearful of being alone and was convinced that someone wanted to hurt her. Although she lived in an apartment complex with elaborate security precautions, she insisted that a group of young boys who hung around the swimming pool in the afternoon had made plans to break into her apartment and rape and kill her. She was so fearful of this that she had insisted that the building superintendent install an extra lock on her apartment door. Even this was not enough, however, and she had installed additional locks on all her doors and windows and had three locks on her bedroom door. She would not go to bed unless all the lights in the apartment were burning. Two weeks before, she had asked the woman across the hall to keep a watch on the apartment all night, as she was certain that an attempt on her life was going to be made that particular night. Even when Woody was at home, she would not sleep in the dark.

Although she described herself as a very lonely person, Sonya refused all invitations from neighbors to become involved in social activities. She was also convinced that Woody was having a number of affairs with other women while he was away from home. Admitting that he had become increasingly frustrated in his attempts to understand and communicate with his wife, Woody said that he had reached the point where he dreaded coming home. When he did try to spend an evening talking or watching television with his wife, he said that she would eventually turn the conversation to his supposed involvement with other women and had sometimes accused him of having homosexual relationships. She had often threatened to expose his extra-marital escapades to his parents, and had gone so far as to call the airline for which he worked and inform them that Woody and one of the stewardesses were having an affair.

When he would try to convince her that he was not involved with other women, she would usually retreat to her bedroom and hide under the covers. The night that she was admitted to the hospital, Woody had been awakened by a banging noise in the back of the apartment. He had gone to the kitchen and found Sonya banging her head against the refrigerator door. When he had tried to restrain her, she had told him about the pills and her desire to die. When she began to scream and fight, Woody had summoned help from neighbors and taken Sonya to the hospital.

In the sessions which followed, the counselor learned that Sonya had never wanted children. Even though he had ceased to pressure her, Woody had continued to hope that she would eventually change her mind. She had instead become even more insistent that she had no desire to have children, and several years earlier she had taken a job as a legal secretary. Although she had become very proficient in her work—her employers constantly praised her—Sonya had quit the job after she had become convinced that her boss and fellow employees were making fun of her. She had more recently taken a job as a part-time hostess and cashier in a small restaurant near her apartment. Even this had become too much for her in recent weeks, however, and she had found herself unable to concentrate or to think straight. As a result, she had become convinced that she had a brain tumor. Even after several physicians had examined her and found no evidence of any physical disorder, she had continued to believe that she was suffering from a brain tumor or lesion. She complained frequently of stomach pains and headaches.

In individual sessions with one of the hospital psychiatrists, it was learned that Sonya had shown signs of emotional problems even as a child. Her parents demanded that she excell, and Sonya had been an excellent student. She had, however, had little social life and had never dated before she entered college. Although as a child she was liked by her teachers and peers, she chose to spend most of her time alone. She was an avid reader and collected comic books by the hundreds, reading and re-reading them for hours on end. Still isolated and alone, she had steadfastly refused to date until she met Woody when she was a senior in college. Woody, six years her senior and recently divorced, had persisted until Sonya relented and dated him. Within two months they were engaged, and they were married two weeks later.

Discussion

Having already cited statistics regarding the break-up of two out of every five marriages, we would like to suggest that another set of statistics be considered as having some bearing on the inability of couples to make a go of it in marriage. We are told that approximately one out of ten people in this country is emotionally disturbed to the point that hospitalization or some form of outpatient treatment is required. These figures do not include the large number estimated to need psychological help who will, for various reasons, never seek such help.

Although we cannot quote numbers to substantiate such claims, our experience in working with couples has led us to conclude that many experience difficulties in marriage as a result of a mental dysfunction on the part of one or both of them. Stated another way, it is our opinion that psychopathology is encountered in both marriage and pre-marriage counseling too frequently to be ignored in any serious analysis of divorce statistics.

Despite the awareness that more people are afflicted with mental and emotional disorders than with all physical disorders combined, mental health and emotional stability are seldom discussed or viewed as matters of great importance in the selection of a mate unless it is blatantly obvious that one of the people suffers from a serious emotional disturbance.

In attempting to discuss the possible relationship between a good marriage and good mental health, we would not be so foolish as to recommend that a person not marry someone suffering from emotional problems any more than we would suggest that poor people or those without college degrees make poor marital partners. After all, there are many good marriages in which one or both spouses has experienced episodes of mental instability. Given enough stress and pressure, every human being has a breaking point.

What we are suggesting is that mental health is just as important as physical health or social standing in the choice of a husband or wife. Most people would not refuse to marry someone they loved if they discovered the person had heart trouble or diabetes. Most would, however, want to know that such a condition existed and would feel deceived if this information were concealed until after the marriage.

While we would stop far short of suggesting that individuals not marry anyone known to be suffering from some form of mental disorder we do believe that good mental health is a valuable asset in a relationship between a man and a woman.

With this in mind, it should be emphasized that all persons contemplating marriage should take every opportunity to get to know each other as well as possible before making the decision to marry. Knowledge about the mental and emotional condition of the person one is considering for marriage is a vital part of getting to know him or her. Certainly this should not be disregarded in a matter as important as choosing a mate for life. Not only should the mental health of the potential spouse be considered; the emotional condition of siblings, parents, and other close relatives can provide significant insights into what might be expected in the future when stress arises or children are born.

If one assumes that there is in many cases a connection between mental illness and failure in marriage, what indicators might suggest the likelihood of serious emotional problems which could prove detrimental to the building of a good marriage?

While this is not a book on abnormal psychology, we can suggest that the presence of symptoms listed below should alert the observer to the possible presence of, or potential for, serious emotional problems.

(1) Long or frequent periods of isolation, withdrawal, or alienation from others.
(2) Extreme difficulty in relating to or communicating with others.
(3) Inability to express feelings or emotions.
(4) Inappropriate behavior or exaggerated responses in most situations.
(5) Tendency to be overly suspicious, sensitive, distrustful, or fearful.
(6) Tendencies toward cruelty or violence toward self, other individuals, or animals.

(7) Frequent and prolonged bouts of depression or anxiety.

(8) Distortion of reality or bizarre and irrational ways of thinking and behaving.

(9) Absence of conscience or sense of wrongdoing.

(10) Drastic and sudden swings in mood without reasonable cause.

(11) Frequent or prolonged disturbances in life functions (i.e., sleeping, eating, working, playing).

(12) Excessive use of alcohol or other forms of drug abuse.

(13) Excessive anger or irritability.

(14) Marked absence of self-confidence.

(15) Frequent or exaggerated physical complaints when no organic cause can be found.

The above are just a few of the symptoms which may be seen in individuals experiencing some emotional stress. If any of these is present, further evaluation is recommended.

marry someone with major religious differences

Joy and Skip, both juniors in college, came for counseling after Skip's parents had informed him the night before that they would no longer support him or pay his college expenses if he continued to date Joy.

When asked why his parents were so opposed to his dating Joy, Skip replied that they were Orthodox Jews, while Joy was a Protestant. He went on to say that he had been told since early childhood that the one thing which his father would never tolerate was the marriage of any of his children to a person outside their faith. According to Skip, his older brother and sister had not disappointed their father and had established what seemed to be good, solid marriages with persons of whom he approved.

Skip stated, however, that while he still believed in God, he had come to the conclusion, after meeting Joy and other non-Jewish college students, that one's religious preference really made little difference as long as respect for others' viewpoints was upheld.

Despite Skip's attempts to reason with him, his father had hit the ceiling when Skip had admitted to him six months earlier that he had been dating Joy. Although at first he insisted that they were in love and that he intended to continue dating Joy, Skip had eventually promised to discontinue the relationship when his father refused to let him bring Joy into the house and threatened to disown him if he ever saw her again.

After a short time, however, Joy and Skip had begun seeing each other again in secret, and had been doing so for three months when a friend of Skip's family saw them together at a ball game and told his father. It was at this time that the first appointment with the counselor was arranged.

In the first session Joy and Skip maintained that their love for each other had grown as a result of the opposition they had endured, and both insisted that they planned to marry when they graduated the next year.

Although they had not been overjoyed when they were told of Joy's love for Skip, her parents had not openly opposed the relationship. Their major complaint had been the constant state of stress which their daughter seemed to be in as a result of her involvement with Skip and the effect the stress was having on her health, both physical and emotional. Despite Joy's loss of weight and difficulty in sleeping, they had refused to take sides in the conflict, emphasizing that Joy and Skip were adults and had to decide for themselves what they wanted to do with their lives.

Skip's father, by comparison, became even more persistent in his disapproval of the relationship and not only forbade Skip even to enter his house, but also said that if he went ahead with the marriage, he would be considered the same as dead by the rest of the family. In apparent agreement with Skip's father, other relatives had severed all connections with Skip and ignored him if they passed him on the street or met him in a restaurant. If he phoned, they were either cold and distant or hung up when they recognized the caller.

Although he said that he was still determined to go ahead with the marriage and had even moved the date up, Skip confessed that the lack of communication between him and his family had caused him much concern and distress. He was also greatly concerned with the effect it was having on Joy, who had changed from a carefree, happy girl to one who seemed moody, despondent, and irritable much of the time. When confronted with this bit of information, Joy admitted for the first time that she was beginning to have second thoughts about the marriage because of her reservations concerning how long they could stand up under such unfair criticism and attacks.

Discussion

Just as a strong religious faith can hold couples and families together when adversity strikes, major differences in this area can destroy a relationship or seriously hamper the chances for its survival, as in the case of Joy and Skip. While there are successful inter-faith marriages, differences in religious beliefs constitute a formidable obstacle in the development of a lasting relationship for many couples and should not be ignored in the selection of a mate.

While there are those who would argue that religion is no longer a relevant issue for couples anticipating marriage, we cannot agree with such a position. It is our contention that a sizable number of marriages encounter major problems as a result of religious differences between the individuals involved. Not only do we maintain that religion can and often does play a major role in the degree of contentment in marriage, even a cursory examination of our records reveals a significant difference in the rate of divorce for couples who profess to be religious and that of those who make no such claim. While this may not be true in other settings, our personal observations lead us to conclude that among couples considering divorce, the number in which both parties have a strong and mutual religious commitment is minuscule compared with the number who are either downright opposed to religious involvement of any sort or are simply uninterested.

In a recent interview with a young physician who was about to be married, he stated that "Couples who fail to include religion as an essential element in their marriage could never know the meaning of marriage in its fullest sense." An older woman, recently divorced, said in a counseling session shortly after her divorce that if she ever married again it would be to a man who shared her faith and commitment to God. She also said that the absence of a shared faith had played a major role in the break-up of her marriage. Still another woman, in the process of divorce, recently made the statement that she knew she was "going against God's will" when she married her husband, who had made no attempt to conceal his lack of interest in religious matters prior to their marriage.

While there are those who would not be impressed with the opinions expressed in the preceding paragraph, in our casework we cannot ignore the number of disintegrating marriages in which the absence of religion or the presence of religious differences seems to be of major significance. Nor can we discount those occasions, in working with couples or families who have experienced the death of a family member, when some remaining member has said that without their religious faith and the strength derived from it, they could not have survived as individuals, as a couple, or as a family.

In a case like that of Joy and Skip, the schism between one partner and his or her family could work to bring them closer together as a couple. On the other hand, in the years ahead it could result in Skip's resentment for having had to pay such a high price for his marriage to Joy.

An inter-faith marriage can become even more complicated if the couple decides to have children. Although many couples obviously work this out to the satisfaction of all involved, others never do.

While spouses of different religious faiths or denominations can have serious difficulties, problems seem to be even more serious when one partner is vitally concerned with religious matters and the other either is uninterested in or against the practice of religion in any form. Complications and disagreements under these circumstances can be endless, not only for the couple, but for the children as well.

While we do not feel it appropriate to suggest that everyone should avoid at all costs marriage to someone with different views on religion, we would say that this issue crops up too often in problem marriages to be ignored. Although there are some people who can tolerate the stresses and strains resulting from such differences, there are many who cannot. Consequently, it is our recommendation that a person with a strong religious commitment who anticipates marriage to one who does not share this faith or enthusiasm ask these questions.

(1) How important are my religious beliefs to me?
(2) If it became necessary, would I be willing to sacrifice these beliefs for the sake of peace in my marriage?
(3) How will our religious differences affect our relationship?
(4) How will our religious differences affect our children?
(5) Are our feelings for each other strong enough to compen-

sate for the things we will have to compromise on before we marry each other?

(6) Could our marriage tolerate the pain of having family members cut off all contact with us if we marry against their wishes?

(7) Is there room—or even willingness—to consider compromise without having to sacrifice beliefs or principles of great importance to me?

(8) If I compromise or sacrifice, will my spouse reciprocate, or will he or she remain rigid and unbending?

(9) What are the chances that at some future date my spouse might grow to resent the things he or she had to give up in order to marry me?

marry someone with whom you have nothing in common

Flo and Art, both twenty-eight, complained after five years of marriage that they no longer enjoyed each other's company and blamed it on a lack of common interests. Although at first both had found it exciting to be married to someone from such a different background, they now found themselves doing almost nothing together. They said that they still cared for each other as people, but both felt that they would eventually divorce and that any attempt to work things out would only postpone the inevitable.

Indicating they had been to marriage counselors before, Flo said that their values were just too different to make the marriage work. As a person who loved to read, she found it difficult to understand how Art could go for weeks without even reading a newspaper. He never read a book and only occasionally looked at a sports magazine. When she tried to talk to him about world affairs or personal values, he refused to engage in such conversation and turned to television instead. When she purchased season tickets to plays and concerts, he refused to accompany her and purchased season tickets for local college basketball games. A great lover of classical music, Flo viewed Art's requests that she listen to country music or watch pro football on television with him as an insult to her intelligence. She was already an accomplished pianist, and she had recently taken guitar lessons. Whenever she sat down to play the piano, however, Art would find an excuse to leave the house and usually ended up drinking beer until midnight with some of his buddies.

Even their taste in friends was so different that they seldom did anything with other couples. An avid sportsman and lover of the outdoors, Art spent many evenings playing softball and basketball and weekends hunting and fishing. Choosing to remain at home rather than participate in such activities, Flo complained of loneliness but said she preferred that to doing something she found distasteful.

Art had majored in agriculture in college. Flo had majored in English and admitted that she felt intellectually superior to Art. She came from a family which placed great emphasis on education and cultural matters, and her parents had from the beginning resented her involvement with Art. They refused to have anything to do with his parents, who had not finished high school. Although she had defended Art in the beginning, Flo said that she could by no stretch of her imagination see herself content to settle down in a small town or on a farm where she would be deprived of the cultural advantages of large cities.

After several sessions with the counselor, Art and Flo decided on a trial separation. They agreed that they were so different that making it together would require more changes than it would be worth. Neither seemed motivated to change or even interested in trying.

Discussion

A lack of common interests is another complaint frequently heard by marriage counselors, and it is one which seems to be high on the lists of reasons given for marital breakdowns. While it is neither possible nor desirable for couples always to share the same interests, having very little in common can lead to serious problems. When a couple finds they are doing nothing together, they will eventually raise the question "Why stay married?"

For many people the prospect of being married to someone from an entirely different background can be very exciting at first. It is not uncommon, for example, to see a gentle and sensitive woman married to a man who is both crude and cruel, or a highly educated man married to a high school drop-out. Often a person with high moral standards ends up married to a person of questionable character, sometimes one with a long history of criminal activities. The possibilities are endless, as any marriage counselor can attest.

While there may be some truth in the belief that opposites attract, it is also important that couples have some desire to share their lives with each other. Since the tendency is to try to impress one's partner while dating, it is often difficult to determine the degree to which individuals have mutual interests.

Many people complain that before marriage their spouses gave the impression that they enjoyed certain activities. After marriage, however, there was a noticeable lack of interest in pursuing those activities shared earlier. Many women, for example, say that while dating, their husbands were very attentive, affectionate, tender, and romantic. They often went to concerts or nice restaurants and did lots of things together. After marriage, however, many wives complain that their husbands have changed, and they wonder if they were ever the way they seemed at all. Husbands likewise complain that their wives gave the impression that they were sincerely interested in sports, sex, travel, company, or myriad other activities which they seemed to have in common until the man was "hooked." When this happens, both husbands and wives end up feeling that they have been tricked or deceived.

Differences in life-styles should be considered when raising the question of compatibility with another person. Life-styles that leave little time for mutual sharing will not enhance a marriage relationship. The following are just a few of the many contrasting life-styles which can drain marriages rather than provide them with sustenance.

(1) The spouse who is a "work-a-holic" vs. the spouse who likes to work from nine to five and have other activities to pursue.

(2) The socialite vs. the home-body. Some people find recreation and refreshment in socializing; others find that the solitude of home enhances their emotional well-being. Both desires are normal, but they are very different.

(3) The spouse who likes a predictable routine vs. the spouse who likes constant variety.

(4) The spouse who wants to socialize primarily with others of the same sex vs. the spouse who enjoys doing things as a couple and with other couples.

marry someone who is easily and frequently bored

Page, a beautiful twenty-eight-year-old hair stylist, and Tripp, a successful thirty-three-year-old dairy farmer, visited a mental health center for marriage counseling because of Page's growing boredom with living on a farm. Although she freely admitted that her husband was a sober, faithful, and responsible breadwinner whom she greatly admired, Page quickly added that she could not spend another year on a farm with only cows for companions.

Out of desperation she had taken a job in a hair salon which catered to both men and women. Although she denied having affairs with any of the male customers, she confessed that she did find their attention flattering. In their small town word soon reached Tripp that his wife was behaving in a fashion most unbecoming to a twenty-eight-year-old woman who was married and the mother of a seven-year-old child.

When Tripp confronted his wife with the rumors, Page had blamed them on village gossip and firmly denied that she had done anything to encourage men to flirt with her. More than once during the session, however, she reminded Tripp in great detail of their own boring life-style and implied that he could not really blame her if she did find offers from other men inviting.

Describing herself as a person who liked excitement, bright lights, parties, lots of attention, and nice clothes, Page was at a loss for words when asked why she had been attracted to Tripp in the first place, since she described him sarcastically as "perfectly satisfied to stay at home and watch the corn grow."

Tripp agreed that he was quite content with farm life and painted a picture of himself as a conscientious, hard-working, and conservative man who enjoyed attending church on Sunday and meeting occasionally with other farmers or local businessmen to discuss cattle or politics. Quite concerned with his reputation and his standing in the community, he admitted that he found stories of his wife's behavior toward other men very offensive. Although he had been attracted to her in the beginning because she was exciting and beautiful, he confessed that he had found it increasingly difficult to keep her satisfied. He had on numerous occasions chastised her for sexually provocative behavior. While still proud of her and appreciative of her physical beauty, he had repeatedly warned her that it was unnecessary to flaunt it in front of everyone or to come on so strong when they occasionally attended social functions in the community.

He was particularly incensed that she seemed to go out of her way to be sexually attractive to other men while often refusing to engage in sexual relations with him. Even when she did, she complained that it was not very enjoyable to her and accused him of being a poor lover.

Tripp also complained that he had had to assume most of the responsibility for the care of their seven-year-old daughter, often preparing her meals, helping her with her homework, and even buying most of her clothes. Page admitted that she found housework and taking care of a child uninteresting and burdensome. When at home with her daughter, she preferred to watch soap operas on television, take sun baths, and read love stories. She did say that she enjoyed going to church on Sunday since this was, in her words, "about the only chance I have to really dress up and be with people."

When the marriage counselor attempted to arrange another appointment, Page refused to return, although her husband expressed a willingness to do so. Insisting that the only thing that might help her was a change of environment, Page told the counselor that she was taking a few weeks off to visit friends in New York and would consider future sessions when she returned.

Discussion

Boredom is one of the major causes of divorce. Couples like Page and Tripp show up for marriage counseling with amazing frequency. While it is difficult to see how such people can be attracted to each other in the first place, they seem to do so in great numbers. Most marriage counselors are all too familiar with the problems generated by the marriage of a rather staid, conservative, and responsible man to an attractive, colorful, fun-loving, and exciting woman. While the man is often a very exacting, detail-minded, serious, and routine-oriented person, the woman is often showy, frivolous, light-hearted, flighty, and outgoing.

Since such people do become involved with each other so often and with such poor results, there is much speculation as to why they are initially attracted to each other. One of the explanations most often heard is that the man is attracted to the woman because she livens things up and provides zest for his rather humdrum existence. On the other hand, the woman, with her carefree qualities and her desire for excitement and variety, can rely on the more dependable, predictable, and responsible man for stability and security. Although such marriages are usually very hectic, some seem to remain intact for these reasons.

Some of the most common characteristics seen in such marriages are listed here. The woman is easily bored. The day-to-day repetition of events inevitable in all marriages is difficult for her to tolerate. She likes to party often and be the center of attention. The husband, on the other hand, derives great satisfaction from doing his work well and enjoys a calmer sort of existence. Husbands in such marriages often complain that they cannot conduct serious conversations with their wives and accuse them of being too shallow.

Sexual problems seem to abound. A common complaint is that while the woman is unusually coy and seductive with men, she often fails to follow through in sexual matters and seems to get little pleasure out of sex itself. The conquest seems more important than the act of sexual sharing itself. Although she may have initiated the sex play and appears to be very excited about the prospect, when the moment of truth arrives, she may run or come up with many reasons why she cannot go through with intercourse.

While the wife complains of being bored, the husband often says that he feels as if he is on a merry-go-round.

Not only do such couples frequently make poor marriage partners, they also often prove to be poor parents. The mother may be too shallow and irresponsible to provide adequate care for a child. She is often so caught up with her own overwhelming need for attention that she may strongly resent having to share the spotlight with a child. Pregnancy itself may be extremely distasteful to such women, since they place a premium on their physical appearance and view the role of parent, with its great responsibilities, as restrictive and demanding.

On the other hand, the father may be too serious in his approach to parenthood. He is very demanding and exacting of himself, and these expectations are often transferred to the child. He may insist, for example, that the child's room be kept unreasonably neat and that toys always be in their proper place. When the child is less than perfect, there may be dire consequences. He or she may be made to feel guilty and inadequate when unable to live up to the rigid and perfectionist demands of the father. Such children often say in later life that they can never recall being praised by their fathers for anything they did.

While such marriages are usually characterized by tumult and dissatisfaction, the initial attraction seems to be strong and the relationship mutually satisfying during the courtship stage. The more serious business of day-to-day living with another person usually proves to be too much, however, and the couple's many differences gradually emerge. Such couples may make it together, but there is often a great deal of unpleasantness and frustration for both of them as well as for their children.

marry someone who never says "I love you"

Barbie and Shane had been married for eleven years and had three children when they went to see a marriage counselor for the first time. Shane was self-employed as an electrical contractor, while Barbie worked on the weekends as a nurse at the local hospital. They had a nice home and lived comfortably on a large farm five miles from town. Both Shane and Barbie were well respected in the community and were active in church and civic affairs. They were considered by friends and acquaintances to have an ideal marriage.

During the first session, Barbie reported that she had gone to her minister the week before and told him that she was seriously considering leaving Shane and taking the children with her. Saddened by this unexpected news, their pastor had suggested that Shane and Barbie seek marriage counseling before making any final decision.

When the marriage counselor asked her to elaborate on her desire to leave Shane, Barbie reported that all the romance had gone out of their relationship. Admitting that Shane was a faithful and hard-working husband who provided well for his family, Barbie said she could no longer live with the feeling that she was unloved and unappreciated. "I don't see myself as a nag," Barbie said, "but unless I pin Shane down and ask him if he still loves me, he never tells me. He hasn't told me in years that he loved me without my prompting him to say it. Even then he usually says, 'You ought to know by now how I feel, and if you don't, then nothing I say will make any difference.' Whenever he takes me out, we take the whole family and go somewhere to eat hamburgers. At Christmas and on my birthday he always gives me a present, but it is usually something like a dishwasher or a vacuum cleaner. I wish that just once he would send me flowers or take me out to a nice restaurant. Most of all I wish he would just tell me he loves me sometimes and show a little affection. He never hugs the children or tells them that he loves them either. Although he spends time with them and is home every night, I feel they also need love and affection from their father."

Although he looked hurt, Shane responded to his wife's comments by saying that she was telling the truth. He also said that he did love his wife and children very much but that he was just not the type to go around hugging people or showing affection. Even as a young boy, Shane said, he had never been one to express his feelings and had never had a really close friend with whom he shared his feelings. On the many occasions when his wife would attempt to get him to understand her need for love and affection, Shane would say, "Actions speak louder than words." He continued to the counselor: "I feel that my love for Barbie should be obvious because of the way I take care of her and the children. I work hard and give them just about everything they ask for. I spend most of my free time with them, and I am usually at home when I'm not working."

Barbie broke in at this point to protest that it was not the amount of time he spent with her that mattered; it was what they did or did not do when together that left her feeling unloved and empty. "Even when we make love," Barbie said, "it is routine, and there is no time for tenderness or affection. Although I don't get much out of sex any more, it is the only time Shane ever holds me or even touches me. If I try to cuddle up next to him on the sofa or even hold his hand while he is watching television, he makes excuses to move apart, saying he has not had time to take a bath yet or that it is too hot to sit close to anyone."

In the weeks following their first visit for counseling, Barbie reported that Shane seemed to be making a sincere effort to be more responsive to her needs for love and affection. Although she appreciated his efforts, she said that it seemed such a strain and so artificial that it still left her feeling cold and unloved.

After several more sessions in which Barbie continued to express disappointment in their relationship, Shane angrily informed her that he was doing the best he could. He concluded by telling Barbie that he did not want her to leave, but that if she could not accept him as he was, he could see no other alternative.

Discussion

The dialogue between Barbie and Shane brings to mind the response of the husband to his wife of twenty-five years when she complained that he never told her that he loved her any more: "I told you before we were married twenty-five years ago that I loved you and that if I ever changed my mind I would let you know."

Although some would say that Barbie's complaints are unjustified and her problem insignificant, they are heard in many sessions with couples. Most if not all people need to feel appreciated and loved. In addition, most want to be told that they are loved and appreciated. There are, however, some who need to have this love demonstrated and verbalized more than others. Like Shane, many persons find it difficult if not impossible to tell another human being that they care for them or love them. This seems especially true for men in our society. While we would not argue with Shane that there are other ways to show love, the fact remains that for many people like Barbie, actions are not enough. At the same time, it is important to remember that not all people need to be reassured that they are loved to the degree that Barbie does.

Since individuals' needs for affection and tenderness do vary so greatly, it is important that differences be recognized and some attempt at a solution be worked on before marriage. If either person is much more demonstrative than the other or exhibits a strong need for love and affection greatly out of proportion to that which the other partner is willing or able to give, then trouble can be anticipated.

In all probability Shane was being truthful when he said that he loved his wife and children very much. There are many people who feel and love very deeply but are unable to express their love in an open or straightforward manner. If one is married to an individual who recognizes and accepts his or her love despite the inability to demonstrate it verbally or with displays of affection, there may be no serious problem. On the other hand, there are people like Barbie who have a strong need not only to be loved but to have this love demonstrated in words as well as deeds. They are demonstrative in their own expressions of affection and expect the same from their mates. For such individuals marriage to someone like Shane can leave significant and powerful needs unfulfilled. The real tragedy is that in many cases the partners do sincerely care for each other, but due to important differences in how they feel love should be expressed, they end up hurt and frustrated.

For the person with strong needs for a partner capable of showing love, tenderness, and attention frequently and openly, it is important to seek answers to some of the following questions.

(1) Does the other person have the desire to respond to my needs in a way which is meaningful to both of us?

(2) If so, is he or she able to respond to my needs in ways which will not cause an unfair burden or strain on either of us?

(3) Does the other person seem uncomfortable and ill-at-ease when attempting to express love and affection verbally or physically?

(4) Does your prospective mate seem threatened by closeness or intimacy?

(5) Does the other person make excuses or find reasons to avoid any manifestation of affection?

(6) Is the other person able to say "I love you," or does he or she take it for granted that I know without being told?

(7) If the latter is true, how do I feel about his or her reluctance to put feelings into words or other obvious forms of expressing affection?

(8) Does the other person feel that any display of love or emotion is a sign of weakness?

(9) Is he or she against any public display of affection?

(10) Is the other person against any display of affection when we are alone?

(11) Is he or she able to express other emotions when they seem appropriate, i.e., crying when sad?
(12) Am I rebuffed when I try to be demonstrative or create an atmosphere for romance?
(13) Does the other person seem ill-at-ease when I talk of love or intimate things?
(14) Is the other person attentive and interested in going places and doing things which he or she knows I enjoy?

In attempting to answer the preceding questions, one should remember that the fulfillment of needs for both individuals is the key to any successful marriage. If important personal needs go unmet for either partner, then frustration and problems are inevitable. While it is impossible for any person to meet all the needs of another human being, it is obvious that Shane failed to meet one of Barbie's most compelling needs. Even though he was a good husband in many respects, hurt and disillusionment were the results of his inability to fulfill that need.

marry someone who is so devoted to his work that he has no time for you

Link, a brilliant and successful thirty-seven-year-old physician, had been married to Addie for eleven years. They had met in the hospital where Addie worked as a nurse. After marriage Addie had stopped work to have children and had never gone back to nursing. With three children, ages four, seven, and nine, she had been satisfied to stay at home. When she had on one occasion expressed a desire to go back to work after all the children were in school, Link had immediately informed her that he wanted her to be there when he came home at night. Content in her role as a mother, Addie had not raised the issue again until the preceding week, when she had told Link that she needed to become involved in something to help fill the many lonely hours she spent while he was working.

Ill-at-ease in the initial session with the marriage counselor, Link demanded that his wife go ahead and explain their reason for being there. When questioned about his obvious reluctance to be there with her, Link said that he had had to cancel a number of appointments in order to make the meeting. On the verge of tears, Addie said that Link had not wanted to come at all and had only done it to pacify her because she had begged him for months to see a counselor with her.

When she was asked to elaborate, Addie began by saying that her husband just never had any time for her or the children. Adding that she was envious of the time he gave to his many patients, Addie remarked that he was held in high esteem—almost worshiped—by them. She said that almost every day someone would stop her on the street or at a meeting to tell her how lucky she was to be married to such a great and compassionate man.

Addie said that she had had some idea what it would be like to be married to a professional person because her father was a minister, but she sobbed that she had never thought it would be this bad. She said that her husband left for the hospial around seven in the morning and that she never knew when to expect him back in the evening. Even when he did return home for dinner, he would eat hurriedly and spend a few minutes with the children while he watched the news. He would then return to the hospital for evening rounds or retire to his study, where he pored over medical journals and books until late at night. He seldom took an entire day off from work. When he did, he would usually play golf or go fishing with other doctors, and they talked shop most of the day.

By this time struggling to maintain her composure, Addie said that the only thing of any real importance to Link was his work. As a result, her needs for attention and affection—as well as those of the children—usually went unmet. She insisted that she could not understand how Link could be so sensitive and responsive to his patients while ignoring his own wife and children, and she added that they went for weeks without having sexual relations. Even when Link took the time to have sex, he did so in a perfunctory manner, seeming to be in a rush to get back to the never-ending practice and demands of medicine. On the rare occasions when he would take the children on an outing or play ball with them, he would seem so impatient and restless that they had told their mother that it was not any fun to have their father around. If he was interrupted by a call from a patient, Link seemed relieved to have an excuse to leave.

Insisting that he did love his family, Link told the counselor that Addie just could not understand how demanding medicine was and how much his patients needed him. When he had tried to explain to her that he needed time each day to read his medical journals to keep abreast of the changes in medicine because it would be unfair to his patients if he failed to do so, Addie had replied, "Your children need you just as much as your patients do. And I'd like to have just one evening alone with you without the phone ringing or your having to rush off to some medical meeting." Interrupting his wife at this point, Link shouted, "Well, you knew what I was like when you married me. You knew how dedicated and ambitious I was."

Addie admitted that Link had always put a lot of time on his studies and work even when they were dating, but she reminded him that he had told her that things would be different after he finished his residency and got out on his own. Rather than their spending more time together, however, Addie said that things had become worse. Agreeing with Addie that he had thought he would have more time for her after his training was over, Link reminded her that he had also told her from the beginning that medicine was the most important thing in his life and that he would never let anything interfere with this love. Turning to Addie, Link said, "I love you and the children, but I don't think I can ever change. While I can understand that you and the children need me, you will just have to understand that I could never be a part-time doctor. I am indebted to you for all you have done to help me finish school and get started in practice, but I do not see how I can give any more of my time to you and still maintain the high standards I have set for myself as a physician. You will have to understand and accept that if we are to stay together."

Discussion

The problem discussed above is so common among people of all classes and vocations that it hardly seems necessary to comment at all. And yet it continues to crop up so often as a major source of controversy in marriage that it is apparent that an astounding number of couples manage to ignore the potential for such conflict. Although before marriage Link had made it quite clear to Addie, both in words and deeds, that she would play a secondary role in his life, she had proceeded with the marriage on the assumption that things would change.

Once again we are confronted with the perennial problem of couples entering marriage with the idea that it will somehow work miracles, and once again we are compelled to remind couples anticipating marriage that if you cannot accept the other person as he or she is during courtship, then you had better think twice before marriage.

Addie's complaint is often voiced by wives as well as children of such dedicated (or indifferent) men, and it seems to occur with great frequency in marriages involving doctors, lawyers, and clergymen. Even though it seems to be an occupational hazard in the aforesaid professions, it strikes marriages involving men and women from all walks of life.

While the lack of time spent with family in the above case is attributed to the demands placed on a physician by his profession, it can also be attributed to other less noble or altruistic causes such as the sheer indifference or insensitivity of one marital partner to the needs of the other. It is not uncommon to hear wives say that their husbands spend all of their time on the golf course or in front of the television set. Whatever the reasons, the complaint remains the same: "No time for me or the children." Nor do all such complaints come from women. With the increasing number of women working outside the home, husbands frequently voice similar complaints. Neither is it uncommon to hear children say, "Mom is so wrapped up in her work that she never has time for us."

While this problem exists among all professions and vocations, it seems most difficult to accept in those families in which the husband is involved in work which requires that he be compassionate and giving to others. Under such circumstances wives often say, "I cannot understand how he can give so much of himself and his time to others and yet neglect his own family." Because he is revered and respected by those he helps, outside observers cannot understand the wife's unhappiness and often accuse her of being selfish and insensitive to both her husband and to the needs of the people he serves. Rather than receiving sympathy, his wife is in many cases expected to sacrifice her own needs and those of the family and devote her efforts to supporting her husband's work.

Men who seem obsessed with the need to work are sometimes referred to as "work-a-holics." Some authorities believe that such men attempt to lose themselves in their work in much the same way that the alcoholic attempts to lose himself in the bottle.

Many such people are afraid of intimate relationships and have great difficulty in expressing love and affection. They manage to get most of their needs for interpersonal contact met through more superficial and less demanding relationships involving their patients, clients, co-workers, students, or congregations. Often they shower their wives and children with gifts and other material things as a substitute for time and affection.

Like the alcoholic, the man who goes far beyond the call of duty—often working eighteen to twenty hours a day with no time off for his family—can change if he sincerely wants to. Like the alcoholic, however, he often has no desire to change.

Since people like Link are often revered as great humanitarians—and frequently do in fact make enormous contributions to society—it is not our intent to suggest that they should be something else. It is important, however, to recognize that marriage to such a person can be unpleasant, even intolerable, unless his or her goals and dedication to duty are shared by the other partner. Many women married to such men involve themselves in a demanding job or get their needs met through club meetings, social and civic functions, or through their children or church.

While marriage to a "work-a-holic" can be most trying for the partner unsuited to such a life, there is usually no excuse for the marriage to have occurred in the first place, since most of these individuals were driven, dedicated, and extremely hard-working long before the marriage ceremony took place.

marry someone who is a perfectionist

Kitty and Bud came for counseling because they said they could not agree on the matter of discipline for their children. Describing his wife as a perfectionist, Bud said, "She expects everyone else to be the same. She insists on having a time and a place for everything." In regard to their two boys, ages nine and twelve, Bud complained that Kitty kept a chart of their duties posted in the kitchen and became furious if they failed to complete them. Just that morning she had returned from grocery shopping and discovered the breakfast dishes still unwashed. She had immediately put their oldest son on a week's restriction of two phone calls each day with a time limit of ten minutes.

Kitty defended her philosophy of rearing children by elaborating on her own childhood. Born into a family where money had never been plentiful, she had learned early in life the value of a dollar. Her father, a strict disciplinarian, had expected his children to work, and work they did. Interrupting his wife, Bud said that his pet peeve was his wife's frequent references to her childhood. "Whenever she gets angry at the boys, she immediately launches into a tirade: 'When I was your age, I was expected to do this or that.' The children have heard the refrain so much by now that they get a pained expression on their faces whenever they hear the familiar opening."

When asked how he felt about the assignment of duties around the house, Bud responded that he too felt that children should have responsibilities, but that he did not believe in monitoring them constantly to see that their work was done as expected. Instead, he said, he advocated responsibility through self-discipline. Rather than having someone jump down their throats about every little job they left undone, he felt that the children would eventually learn that they would not eat unless the dirty dishes were washed. If their parents stuck to their guns and refused to step in and supervise the work or do it for them, they would eventually do the tasks themselves.

Describing himself as a less structured person, Bud said that he did not become upset if the house was not always clean or the lawn mowed. He preferred instead that the family spend less time doing work around the house and more time playing or taking trips together.

While she insisted that she also liked to have fun, Kitty said that she could only enjoy playing after all the work had been completed. Operating on the philosophy "We have to live in this house together," Kitty said, "I believe that we should all recognize that certain jobs have to be done whether we like them or not, and the sooner we pitch in and get them done, the quicker we can do the things we enjoy doing. I admit I believe in running a tight ship, but when things are in a state of disarray around the house, or if duties are performed haphazardly, I am miserable. Even though I love Bud dearly, living with him is a constant hassle. He never picks up after himself. While I find it necessary to plan things in advance, he is unpredictable and may decide on the spur of the moment to take a trip. I quit asking friends over from work because I never knew what condition I would find the house in when I got there. The last few times I invited friends to accompany me home, I was embarrassed to death when we walked in and found dirty dishes still on the table and clothes all over the bathroom floor. Bud was barefooted and had on a dirty old pair of pants. Sometimes I don't think he would ever change clothes unless I told him to."

Citing a number of things about Bud which irritated her, Kitty concluded the session by saying that his refusal to back her up when she disciplined the children upset her more than anything else. Agreeing that they often fought about this, Bud said that he had tried over the years to go along with his wife in an effort to present a united front in their child-rearing practices. As the children grew older, however, and began to think more for themselves, he found it increasingly more difficult to agree with his wife's approach toward work, discipline, and punishment.

Bud admitted that conflict between parents in regard to discipline could lead to problems and concluded by saying, "I know how hard it is for them because I know how difficult it is for me to live by the book. I too sometimes want to rebel against Kitty's insistence on doing everything a certain way and at a certain time. I can understand why the boys at times resent her authoritarian and dogmatic approach in her relationship with them. If she could just learn to relax and not be so rigid, we'd all be a lot happier. After all, keeping a clean house is not the most important thing in the world, and yet Kitty becomes frantic if everything is not spotless all the time. She is constantly fussing at me and the boys because we don't keep things as neat as she wants them."

Discussion

Although Kitty and Bud present their major problem as one of disciplining their children, it soon becomes apparent that there are basic personality differences between Bud and Kitty themselves. While they may be experiencing problems in regard to the disciplining of their children, it is possible that focusing on the children enables them to avoid significant conflicts which exist between them as a couple. Indeed, as they go along, they talk about other problem areas (different ideas as to how a house should be run, chores performed, etc.), which strongly suggests that this is probable.

We do not intend to minimize the many problems which can arise in regard to child-rearing practices. The problems involved in rearing children are monumental at best and can result in major conflicts between the parents themselves as well as between children and parents.

Since this is such an important matter, couples anticipating marriage should explore in great detail their philosophies or approaches to rearing children. Areas covered in such an examination should involve as many issues and concerns as possible. The most basic question which couples should raise before marriage is, of course, that of whether or not they both want to have children and, if so, how many and when. If there are major disagreements, then the marriage itself should be questioned.

If the couple is in basic agreement about having children, then other significant concerns should be explored and may involve issues ranging from the role and responsibility of each parent in the family to matters of discipline or religious and moral training. While most couples will never be in total agreement, it is important that they agree on issues which are of great importance to either of them. For example, the matter of where the children will go to church may be of little concern to parents who have no interest in church. On the other hand, it can turn into a real battleground if one of the parents has a strong religious faith while the other professes to be an atheist. In a recent session in which a couple was discussing the imminent birth of their first child, the husband said that he was an atheist and that the thought of sending his child to church to be exposed to ideas which he viewed as untenable was repulsive. The wife, on the other hand, said that her faith in God was the most important thing in her life and that she had no intention of letting her children grow up without religious training.

Another problem area touched on by Kitty and Bud is the difference in needs for structure, organization, orderliness, and neatness. It is amazing how many couples come to counseling with the complaint that they can never agree on the way a house should be kept. A young wife said recently that her husband's sloppy habits nearly drove her up the wall. "Since he works nights, he is home all day. When I come home in the evening, I have to push things aside to find a place to sit or clear off the table before I can have a cup of coffee. He leaves dirty dishes in the sink, ashtrays running over throughout the house, and dirty clothes wherever he takes them off." A minister related, in still another case, that he was ashamed to bring members of his church to his home because his wife was such a sloppy housekeeper and poor hostess. While he confessed that they fought over other issues, he indicated that this was the major source of discord. His wife felt that she had more important things to do with her time than sweeping floors or washing dishes.

As with the matter of discipline, differing ideas as to how a house should be run can in themselves lead to major disruption. In addition, they can be indicative of other more basic personality differences. A successful businessman said in one session, "Our

house looks like a freight train ran through the living room."
When his wife asked him why it was so important to have
everything neat and organized all the time, he replied, "I can tell
a lot about people by the way they keep their homes or busi-
nesses. To me, chaotic and sloppy housekeeping habits suggest
chaos in other areas of a person's life. People who run their
homes in an orderly fashion are probably organized and effective in other areas of their lives." Infuriated, the wife—
recognized as a creative and interesting teacher of high school
seniors—replied, "If I applied your thinking about organization
to my teaching, my students would be asleep most of the time."

Obviously there are no right or wrong answers to such issues,
as illustrated in the exchange above. The important thing is that
two people with such differing viewpoints are trying to live in the
same house, and consequently there is much disruption. Additional sessions revealed that Bud and Kitty differed not only in
their needs for neatness and organization, but in other significant
ways as well. As marriage counselors have learned, conflict over
small and insignificant things in marriage may well be a cover-up
for more serious problems and differences. While such differences can counterbalance each other in some cases, some couples
find life together under such circumstances intolerable.

In general, it might be said that if couples disagree frequently
and violently over small issues before marriage, they are apt to
disagree even more on important issues after marriage. The real
problem is due not so much to the issues they disagree on as to
the inability to resolve the conflict or reach a compromise position
which both can accept. While most couples are able to come up
with a workable solution, there are those such as Kitty and Bud in
whom attitudes and behaviors are so deeply entrenched that
change is most difficult. Many couples manage to ignore major
differences while dating or expect everything to work out after
marriage. Unfortunately, these differences often lead to open
and sometimes violent disagreement after marriage. Neither the
process of marriage nor the passage of time seems to dilute the
anger or frustration of partners locked into such differing life-
styles.

ignore the importance of dollars and cents in marriage

Ron and Caroline could not stop arguing about a sofa. The only one she had found that she liked cost $1500. Ron's yearly income was $11,000, and he felt that the sofa was much too expensive. But Caroline refused to settle for less.

The Bridgeses have both worked full time since their marriage three years ago. Mr. Bridges' income was enough to support them, so they agreed that Mrs. Bridges would put all her salary in savings for crises or luxuries. When the couple recently had emergency expenses, he asked her to withdraw some of her savings. She refused on the grounds that it was "her" money and told her husband to borrow what they needed from a lending company.

Mr. J. earns only enough to provide his family with necessities, yet he often buys his wife extravagant gifts. He is now deep in debt. A somewhat rigid person, he can't understand why his wife doesn't appreciate the presents, although she has told him over and over that she does not want "things" but would rather he showed some affection for her.

Discussion

One of the major emotional battlegrounds in marriage is money. It has been our experience in counseling that couples who have serious financial problems are often in difficulty not because of need or inadequate income. In most cases they have immature or unrealistic attitudes about money, or they use money as a weapon or as a compensation for inadequacies. Many couples overspend because they want all their luxuries at once, they are status-conscious, or they need the ego-bolstering of owning expensive items.

For Ron and Caroline, a stalemate over a sofa was an indication of their inability to resolve their differences. To Mrs. Bridges, money became a means of displaying her own independence. Mr. J. gave his wife expensive gifts as a substitute for the love he was unable to express in any other way. These examples demonstrate how family finances do become a means for spouses to act out feelings that they fear or don't want to face directly.

If there are conflicts over financial matters before marriage, the conflicts are apt to increase after marriage when attempts are made to come to terms regarding joint expenditures and savings. In many cases conflicts are not a question of dollars and cents but of emotions, attitudes, and habits.

If differences exist in fiscal matters, it would be appropriate to raise the following questions.

(1) Can we sit down together and work out a budget which is satisfactory to both?

(2) Can we agree on what is to be done with any surplus money after the bills are paid?

(3) If either wants to purchase something for which no money is available, can we come to some agreement?

(4) How do we both feel about going into debt?

(5) Do we think of income as "ours" or "mine"?

(6) Do we dole out or withhold money as a weapon?

(7) Does either partner consistently wreck the budget in an attempt to get back at the other partner?

(8) Is one partner more skilled in handling money matters? Are we willing to let him or her assume major responsibility in that area?

potpourri

In the preceding pages we have attempted to share with you some of the problems which seem to occur most often in troubled marriages. We are aware, however, that we have not been able to cover all of the problems which can lead to separation and divorce. We would therefore like to present in capsule form other types of problems which often lead to serious conflicts in marriage. Though not heard with the frequency of those mentioned above, they do come up often enough to warrant some discussion.

We have also attempted to demonstrate that in most cases the conflicts experienced after marriage were present prior to marriage. As before, we would suggest that you proceed with caution if your girlfriend or boyfriend seems to fall into any of the categories discussed below.

The Philanderer

There are some people who seem incapable of maintaining a lasting and meaningful relationship with one person. Going outside the marriage, they move from one affair or one-night stand to another when their partners refuse to give them a divorce. Others seem interested in holding on to one person at the center of their lives while having an endless number of affairs outside the primary relationship. Although they insist on this right for themselves, such people are often humiliated if their partners demand the same right.

To such individuals fidelity after marriage often seems unnecessary or undesirable. Traditionally we have tended to think of this behavior as more apt to occur in males (thus the terms Don Juan, Casanova, playboy). In recent years, however, there has been a noticeable increase in women who express similar interests. Without our going into the causes, suffice it to say that for many, such behavior leads to serious problems after marriage.

The Person Without a Conscience

There are some people who seem to engage in all kinds of immoral and unlawful activities without any feelings of guilt or awareness that they are hurting others or disobeying the law. One young wife recently reported that her husband lied to her constantly, stole merchandise from various stores, had affairs with other women, and frequently ignored promises he made to their children. If caught and confronted, he would always come up with an excuse for his behavior or act as if he had done nothing wrong. If he was prodded into saying "I'm sorry" or "I was wrong," he would turn around and repeat the same behavior again in a matter of hours or days. "He just doesn't seem to care anything at all about what is right or wrong," his wife said.

The Person Who Is Always Criticizing

No matter how much you try, some people are never satisfied. We are all familiar with the story of the grumpy old man who said, "I'm going home tonight and if my dinner isn't ready, I'm gonna raise hell with my wife. And if it is, I'm not gonna eat a bite." Some people seem happiest when criticizing others. Marriage to such a person is one big put-down, and both spouse and children suffer the consequences. Children from such marriages often say, "I could never do anything right in my parents' eyes. They never once praised me or told me I did a good job. If I got nineteen questions right on a test, they focused on the one I missed."

The Hypochondriac

One man in a recent session said, "My wife has been to doctors sixty times in the last two years and has been told by every one of them that there is nothing physically wrong with her."

People who are always complaining of physical ailments for which no organic cause can be found need counseling. Unfortunately, this type of person is often reluctant to seek help even when a physician recommends it. They resent being told that their problems are "all in their heads." If they do come for counseling, they often reveal a lack of self-confidence, loneliness, anxiety, and depression in addition to their physical complaints.

In many cases their physical symptoms may be interpreted as their way of getting attention. Since they have such poor self-images, they cannot imagine that anyone could possibly be interested in them for positive reasons.

While occasional sickness may arouse feelings of caring and comfort from a partner, constant complaints or psychosomatic ailments can arouse hostility and resentment.

The Person Who Keeps All Feelings Locked Inside

These individuals may display many of the same characteristics as the hypochondriac: depression, anxiety, low self-esteem, loneliness, pessimism, headaches, stomach problems, skin rashes, and a host of other physical symptoms. They are often reluctant to ask for anything because of their fear of being turned down or rejected. They may insist that they never get angry, and if they do, they see any expression of anger as wrong or as a sign of weakness. They often have difficulty in expressing other emotions as well. They can be very rigid, perfectionistic, pessimistic, and demanding both of themselves and of others. They may have acquaintances but none in whom they confide.

Because they do keep their feelings locked inside, they often develop physical problems such as stomach ulcers, skin rashes, and headaches, and they can become seriously depressed. Although they may get some attention with their complaints, most people soon tire of hearing them. Since they are generally very rigid, however, such people find it hard to change their behavior.

The Person Who Can't Say No

These individuals also share many of the characteristics listed in the two previous categories. Their inability to say no often stems from a poor self-image. They may feel—or even say—"I don't have many friends, so I can't risk losing the few I have by saying no." As a consequence, they often engage in behavior which they find unpleasant, even distasteful, simply because someone else wants them to. Not free to express their feelings, they suffer in silence.

They are usually very compliant people who will do anything to keep from hurting someone else or to avoid a conflict. They sometimes mask their real feelings of insecurity and worthlessness under the guise of service to God or mankind and may say, "My main goal in life is to live for others." Their efforts are directed toward pleasing others. They give generously of themselves but rarely ask for anything.

The Person with Low Self-Esteem

A person's self-image affects everything he or she does in life. A negative self-image may be reflected in many ways. Some people withdraw as much as possible from all human contact. Some reach out in desperation to others, seeing themselves as empty shells unless another person gives some meaning and purpose to their lives. Such individuals, feeling too insecure to make it on their own, may attach themselves to another person for sustenance. Individuals involved with such persons may find themselves in a relationship in which they are constantly called upon for reassurance. Even this may not be enough, however, and the stronger partner may come to see the other as a bottomless pit and retreat from his or her demands in great haste.

The Pessimist

Persons in this category always expect the worst out of life. Their outlook is permeated by gloom and dejection. They usually do not have much faith in themselves or in humanity in general. Marriage to such an individual can be very draining and burdensome.

The Loner

These individuals refrain from most social contact. They often distrust people or feel that people are not interested in them. They may feel more comfortable with animals than with people or prefer work which does not involve people. Problems in marriage arise if one partner is a loner and the other prefers social interaction.

The Person with Unrealistic Views of Love and Marriage

Many people go into marriage expecting to maintain the "high" (or state of euphoria) they experienced in the earlier stages of their relationship. As these feelings begin to wane, they conclude that they are no longer in love. Their concept of love does not go beyond excitement, physical stimulation, stardust, and pleasure. For them marriage is expected to be one gigantic orgasm. For such individuals, problems begin once the honeymoon is over.

The Manipulator

A middle-aged woman reported that she had married her husband sixteen years earlier because he had threatened to kill himself if she stopped dating him. A young man admitted that he had not married his wife because he loved her, but because she made him feel guilty by reminding him of how much of her time he had taken up in the two years they had dated.

Manipulation can be practiced in many ways. One of the most extreme and yet fairly common forms is that of threatening suicide. No matter what form it takes, the person who is manipulated usually resents it. To enter a marriage under these circumstances is in most cases to doom it to failure from the beginning. While the threat of suicide is an obvious manipulative tactic, some individuals' methods are so subtle that their victims may never realize that they have been manipulated.

The Super-Responsible Person

In this group we find people who feel they must solve all the problems of the world. They may, for example, assume responsibility for their parents' poor marriage, the welfare of their brothers and sisters, or for the well-being of anyone who comes to them with a problem.

Such people are often overly conscientious, overly sensitive, and more in contact with the needs and feelings of others than with their own. They may, in truth, be seeking to avoid their own feelings and needs by concentrating so intently on the needs of others. For this type of person, self-awareness and self-expression can be very threatening.

The Person Who Is Not Ready for Marriage

We see many individuals who are convinced that their girlfriends or boyfriends no longer love them. In many cases it soon becomes apparent that the main problem has nothing to do with love but with readiness for marriage. Admitting that they do love their partners, many people tell us that they are not yet ready to commit themselves to marriage and to accept the responsibility for rearing a family.

To pressure anyone into marriage before he or she is ready is asking for trouble in the future.

A Person Whose Educational Level Is Significantly Different from Your Own

This is a problem which is quite common among college students: one spouse is pursuing a college degree while the other is the primary means of financial support. The difference in educational levels seems especially crucial if the working spouse has only a high school education or less. It becomes even more critical when the spouse in college reminds the other of these differences and implies that they can no longer communicate well as a result. Often a working spouse feels devastated when the student spouse decides after graduation that he or she wants a divorce. Such feelings are often expressed in college counseling centers by the working spouse, who feels used and then discarded and often develops feelings of inferiority and resentment.

Persons Who Expect a Spouse to Take Care of Them

Marriage with the expectation that one person is going to take care of another person and protect him or her from life is not realistic. It is easy to see why many people find such expectations intolerable and run for the nearest exit when faced with such a responsibility. While such dependency on another can be expected in children, it can lead to disaster in marriage. The more independent spouse may end up feeling overwhelmed; the dependent spouse may feel betrayed, unloved, and helpless when his or her partner is unable to live up to such unrealistic expectations.

The Person Who Marries to Please Parents

The desire to have grandchildren is quite common. It is not unusual to hear couples say that they are getting pressure from their parents to "go ahead and marry so you can give us grandchildren before we are too old to enjoy them." Yielding to such pressures can result in couples' marrying and starting families before they are ready. Parents may urge their grown children to marry by using reminders such as, "You are not getting any younger," "All your classmates are married except you," and "People are beginning to wonder about you." One single woman in her mid-twenties recently said that she had decided not to attend any more family functions because she was tired of prying relatives constantly asking her when she was going to get married and start having babies.

The Person Who Marries Because It Is Expected

While this is similar to the previous category, pressures here come not only from the family but from society in general. Although there have been some changes in recent years, our society is still basically couples-oriented. People who choose to remain single are often left out, even ostracized. One twenty-nine-year-old man said that if you are not married at his age, people begin to look at you with suspicion. On more than one occasion, he said, he had been asked—in a joking fashion—if he was gay.

The Person Who Marries for Prestige

Marriage counselors are familiar with persons who complain that their spouses have been a disappointment to them because they have not lived up to their potential in their careers or accomplishments. One woman, after ten years of marriage, reported that she could no longer respect her husband and felt that he had deliberately deceived her. He had been a pre-med student when she married him, and she had felt put down when he graduated and entered training to be a lab technician instead of a doctor. Rather than becoming a member of the country club and enjoying the life of leisure she had anticipated, she had to take a job in a department store when the bills began piling up.

On the other hand, some people who do marry persons in the more prestigious professions such as medicine often feel hurt and angry when they discover that the demands placed on professionals often leave them with little time or energy to spend with their families.

CHAPTER 3.

sizing up your chances for a good marriage

It has been our purpose throughout this book to offer couples preparing for marriage a view of concrete issues which should be given some thought before they commit themselves to living together forever. We have done this by sharing with you recurring problems which couples who are already married have identified as trouble spots. The difficulties existed between these men and women before they were married. It is our contention that if they had given some attention to these problems prior to marriage and decided how to handle them, many of the couples might never have needed counseling, and some of the couples heading for divorce might not have married.

Human beings have a remarkable ability to adapt to new situations. The primary mechanism which aids us in adapting is the intelligence to anticipate what may lie ahead from observations, feelings, and past experiences. However, the excitement and elation of courtship often overshadow our awareness of how well we get along with an intended spouse and conflicts or clues of potential problems that are present. Add to this the expectation that "once we're married it will all work out," and you have laid the groundwork for unresolved problems to brew. Conflicts in a relationship work out because the people involved make an effort to find solutions. It's no different before marriage than afterwards. The marriage license does not alter how well two people get along with one another.

Certainly the best preparation for a satisfying marriage is getting to know your partner, not just in the sharing of romantic love, but in the areas which will come to play a major role in the day-to-day experience of living with another person. This is not to say that love is not an important and fundamental ingredient in a marriage, but it can fade quickly if not nurtured with care by the man and woman who share it.

In this chapter we have compiled a list of questions which we consider to be important for those contemplating marriage. It is our belief that if a couple can freely and openly discuss these questions, this experience in itself will go a long way toward building the foundation for a satisfying marriage. We have chosen the following categories because they are areas which have repeatedly come up as major sources of conflict among couples we have counseled with over the years. We suggest that both partners answer the questions individually and then discuss their responses with one another. If there is any question you are unsure of, you are reluctant to answer honestly, or you become aroused about, this is in all probability an issue you and your future mate need to discuss together before you marry.

I. Expression of Love and Affection

1. How does your partner express feelings toward you?
2. Does your partner demonstrate caring in ways that are meaningful to you?
3. Does your partner show love and affection by physical contact such as hugging, kissing, and touching?
4. Does your partner freely share intimate thoughts and feelings with you as an expression of caring?
5. Does your partner even seem hesitant or embarrassed to express love and affection to you?

II. Sex

1. Do you and your partner seem to be relaxed and comfortable in physically intimate situations?
2. Does your partner have a healthy attitude about sex, or does he or she consider it something dirty and undesirable?
3. Does your partner seem unduly troubled by physical appearance or bodily functions?

4. Does your partner become upset whenever sexual matters are discussed?
5. Do you or your partner become upset or feel excessive guilt if sexual petting or sexual intercourse is attempted?
6. If sexual intercourse is attempted, does your partner have trouble responding?
7. Does your partner feel guilty about sexual fantasies or masturbation?
8. Does your partner express (verbally or non-verbally) any interest in having sexual relations with members of the same sex?
9. Does your partner come from a background which is overly restrictive about sexual matters?
10. Does your partner seem interested in practices such as group sex and swapping partners?
11. Does your partner seem unduly embarrassed about his or her genitals, masturbation, sexual curiosity or exploration?
12. What turns your partner on sexually?
13. Does your partner seem reluctant or unconcerned about discussing birth control and the method which is most suitable for the two of you?
14. When does your partner seem to have the most intense sexual desires?
15. Does your partner share feelings and thoughts with you in physically intimate situations?
16. Is there anything about your partner's sexual feelings and behavior toward you that you find distasteful in any way?
17. Does your partner initiate physical contact more or less than you do?

III. **Religion and Morals**

1. What are your partner's religious beliefs?
2. What role do religious beliefs play in your daily lives?

3. How open is your partner to accepting your religious beliefs if there are differences?
4. Can you and your partner discuss your religious beliefs with each other?
5. Do you find it difficult to accept any of your partner's religious feelings or beliefs?
6. How do you feel about the manner in which your partner does or does not practice his or her religious beliefs?
7. Is you partner's family devoutly religious?
8. Is your partner's religion different from yours?

IV. Finances

1. Do you know what your partner's income is?
2. Does your partner discuss money matters easily and freely with you?
3. Does your partner seem overly concerned about money?
4. Does your partner seem unconcerned about money?
5. Does your partner know how to budget money without excessive denial of pleasure or going too far into debt?
6. Is your partner secretive about money and business affairs?
7. Is your partner interested in how you feel about money?
8. If you were married, would you and your partner have an income adequate to support both of you?
9. Do you dislike any of your partner's spending habits?
10. Does your partner dislike any of your spending habits?
11. How do you decide about purchases, whether small or large?
12. What are your financial plans—for the immediate future as well as for a longer term (say five years)?

13. If you plan to accept any financial assistance—either in gifts or money—from one or both of your families after marriage, how do you feel about this, and how do you plan to handle it?

V. Attitudes Toward Relatives

1. How does your partner get along with your family?
2. How does your partner feel about your family?
3. How does your partner get along with and feel about his or her own family?
4. How much time does your partner spend with his or her family?
5. How does your partner's family feel about you?
6. Have you met your partner's family? If not, why?
7. Does your partner seem overly dependent on family in any way?
8. How do you feel about your partner's relationship to family?
9. Do you feel your partner's family does or could interfere in any way with your relationship as a couple?

VI. Children and Child-Rearing Practices

1. How does your partner feel about having children?
2. How many children would your partner like to have?
3. At what point in your marriage would your partner like to have children?
4. How was your partner treated as a child?
5. How does your partner feel about the manner in which he or she was reared?
6. Are you or your partner unable to have children for any reason?
7. Are you and your partner in reasonable agreement as to how children should be reared?

VII. Personal Habits and Conduct

1. How do you feel about your partner's personal appearance, that is, dress, cleanliness, hair, etc.?

2. How do you feel about your partner's manners when you are alone as a couple as well as when you are with other people?
3. If your partner drinks or smokes or uses other drugs, how do you feel about these habits?
4. How do you feel about your partner's eating habits?
5. Do any of your partner's personal habits embarrass you when you are alone together or when you are with other people?
6. How do you feel about the reactions of other people to your partner?
7. Does your partner have any mannerisms which are irritating to you?
8. What kind of housekeeper is your partner?

VIII. **Interests**

1. What are your partner's interests, hobbies, etc.?
2. Do you and your partner have any common interests?
3. Does your partner feel free to share his or her interests with you?
4. Do you have any objections to any of your partner's interests?
5. Do any of your partner's interests cause conflicts in your relationship?
6. Is your partner respectful of your interests, and does he or she show a desire to share any of them?
7. Does your partner seem so involved in work and outside interests that it often feels as though there is little time for you as a couple?

IX. **Openness and Honesty in the Relationship**

1. Do you ever feel that your partner is putting on an act or masking real feelings toward you?
2. Does your partner seem to be comfortable in expressing both positive and negative feelings to you?
3. Does your partner ever appear reluctant to express

feelings that might "hurt" you, make you "angry," or "disappoint" you?

4. Is your partner honest about admitting a mistake, even though it may be embarrassing?
5. Do you feel that your partner is always "putting his best foot forward" when you are together?

X.   Roles of Husband and Wife

1. What tasks would you expect your partner to perform at home if you were married?
2. What roles would you hope your partner could fill in your everyday living together?
3. Do you expect your partner to work after marriage?
4. Do you expect your partner to provide all or part of the income?
5. How do you feel about your partner's having a career?
6. Do you have any misgivings about the work role your partner wants to perform after marriage?
7. What are your and your partner's expectations of the roles of husband and wife?
8. How do you feel about the manner in which your partner's parents perform husband and wife roles?

XI.   Individual Freedom and Personal Growth

1. Does your partner ever appear jealous of time you spend with others such as family and friends?
2. Do you and your partner feel you must spend as much time as possible together in order to secure your relationship?
3. Does your partner seem to feel comfortable about time you want to spend alone or with others rather than feeling that your relationship will suffer?
4. Does your partner encourage your growth and development as an individual?
5. Does your partner have fixed ideas about how he or she wants you to behave when you are together?

6. How does your partner feel about your job or career plans?

XII. Goals as a Couple

1. When and where do you plan to marry?
2. Where do you plan to live after marriage?
3. What are your educational and/or employment plans for the first few years of marriage?
4. What commitments have you made to one another regarding your living together as a married couple?
5. How do you plan to spend your leisure time as a couple?

XIII. Personal Attitudes

1. How willing is your partner to admit mistakes without fearing your response or feeling insecure?
2. How tolerant is your partner of mistakes you make?
3. How accepting is your partner of the mistakes of others such as family, friends, neighbors, and fellow employees?
4. How do you and your partner settle differences?
5. How much do you trust your partner?
6. Do you respect your partner?
7. How does your partner go about making decisions?
8. Can you depend on your partner to hold down a job and follow through on commitments made to you?

XIV. Physical and Mental Health

1. Is your partner moody?
2. Are your partner's moods unpredictable?
3. Is your partner in good spirits most of the time?
4. How does your partner handle anger?
5. How does your partner handle elation?
6. How does your partner handle fatigue?
7. How does your partner handle unexpected situations and problems?
8. What are your partner's emotional hang-ups?

9. What kind of physical condition is your partner in?
10. Does your partner have any habits which are or have the potential to be physically harmful?
11. Do you or your partner have any physical handicaps? If so, how open are you and your partner about feelings regarding the handicap and any limitations it imposes?

CHAPTER 4.

how to improve your chances for a good marriage

How does one keep from committing "marital suicide"? "There is no such thing as a good marriage," some cynics insist; therefore, they ask, "Why spoil a beautiful relationship by marrying?" Living in an age which some critics label as an era of hopelessness and meaninglessness, we are told that the increasing divorce rate is just another indication that marriage and family life as we know them are on the way out.

We are more optimistic about the future, but we too are concerned about the ever-increasing divorce rate and what it means for generations now living as well as for those yet to come. We are concerned because we believe that a society in which so little value is placed on strong family and marital ties cannot exist for long.

Although we agree that the current state of affairs is cause for concern, we must point out that as of yet no one has been able to come up with a satisfactory alternative to marriage. As evidence we cite the large number of previously married and divorced persons who remarry, as well as the vast number who marry each year for the first time—with such great expectations.

Many have explored other avenues in their quest for ways to increase their chances for success in marriage. One proposed solution is "trial marriage": a couple lives together before marrying to see if they are compatible. This too seems to have failed. Recent statistics indicate that the divorce rate is just as high if not higher among those who lived together prior to marriage. The pain and disillusionment are often just as great when the breakup occurs, even if the couple never married. While it may be a good experience for some, others are not so fortunate. Resentment, guilt, children with unwed parents, abortions, and feelings of being used are often postscripts to such relationships.

Where then lies the answer to the ever-mounting problem of divorce?

While we know that couples love, marry, and live happily ever after only in fairy tales, we do believe that people have considerable control over their destinies and that there are some things which can be done to promote better marriages.

With the desire to provide some helpful suggestions for those not yet married, we have again turned to couples we have counseled with in the past. Rather than focusing on problems in their marriages, however, this time we have looked for those strengths or ingredients which seem to enable some couples to maintain a satisfying relationship.

While there is no single list of prerequisites which all agree on, these are some of the qualities most frequently offered as being of primary importance in the selection of a husband or wife.

Qualities to Look for in a Wife or Husband

(1) *Choose someone who has a realistic view of marriage.* Marriage is never a rose garden. It is the most difficult job in the entire field of human endeavors. One of the major causes of failure in marriage might well be the disenchantment suffered by couples when their marriages do not live up to the highly romanticized and unrealistic view perpetuated by Hollywood. While there is a place for love and romance in marriage, these can fade quickly in light of the everday stresses and responsibilities of living with another human being.

(2) *Choose someone who is able to forgive.* The person who is unable to forgive or who holds grudges for long periods of time can turn marriage into a nightmare. We frequently hear individuals in therapy say, "My wife will never let me forget that I made a mistake. Every time she gets mad, she throws it in my face."

Forgiveness is both good theology and good psychology. It is absolutely essential in marriage. Since all human beings make mistakes, the willingness to say "I'm sorry" and "I forgive you" is of utmost importance. It is also important to remember that forgiveness goes both ways. Not only should one be willing to forgive the errant spouse; he or she should also be able to accept forgiveness. Some people find it harder to accept forgiveness for themselves than to forgive others.

(3) *Choose someone who encourages you to grow as an individual.* A young woman recently said, "My husband is always telling me that if I really loved him, I would give up all this garbage about personal growth and devote my time and efforts to making him happy. If I ever express any ideas or needs contrary to his, he gets very upset and tries to make me feel guilty and disloyal."

How often we hear such complaints in marriage counseling sessions! They have become quite common among women in recent years because of the emphasis on women's rights. Unfortunately, many husbands who find such changes hard to accept only drive their wives further away with their possessiveness and their insistence that a wife's needs and feelings should be secondary to those of her husband.

It is our opinion that a marriage cannot grow unless both individuals in the relationship are able to grow also. For this reason it is important that you choose a partner who respects you as an equal and recognizes you as a person with needs which may not always coincide with his or hers.

(4) *Choose someone with a religious faith compatible with your own.* While there are those who would insist that religion is not a major factor in their personal lives or in their marriages, we cannot escape the fact that statistics show that the divorce rate among those professing a strong religious faith is much lower than among those who are not practicing members of a church or religious body.

(5) *Marry someone who knows how to fight constructively.* Since conflict is inevitable in marriage, it is essential that couples learn to handle their differences openly and constructively. Anger is a human emotion—though some insist that the expression of anger is sinful and is not permissible if you really love someone. Even Jesus expressed his anger on occasions. The person who keeps feelings inside or runs away from problems is laying the

groundwork for personal problems as well as problems in marriage. We repeat that if a marriage is to succeed, it is just as important to learn how to fight as to learn how to love.

(6) *Marry someone whose needs for intimacy, warmth, sharing, love, and affection are in keeping with your own needs.* We again emphasize compatibility because of the great variability among individuals regarding the intensity and the satisfaction of these important needs. It can be devastating, for example, if an individual with a strong need for affection marries someone who is unable to express such feelings. On the other hand, if both partners prefer a minimum of expression in this area, they may live together in harmony for many years. Although some would insist that such a marriage would be intolerable, we must recognize that one person's pleasure may be another's poison.

(7) *Choose someone who is reasonably mature.* Under this category we would include such key attributes as dependability, responsibility, loyalty, trustworthiness, patience, tolerance, and kindness to others.

(8) *Marry someone who can discuss problems openly when they occur.*

(9) *Marry someone who is flexible.* People do change. It is unrealistic to expect the person you marry—or yourself—to be exactly the same person ten years after marriage.

(10) *Marry someone who tends to express ideas and feelings in ways you find acceptable.* We often hear husbands and wives complain that one is always rational and logical in his or her approach to life, while the other is very emotional and impulsive. Ideally, individuals would recognize the importance of both ideas and feelings in their dealings with each other. Unfortunately, they do not always do so. While some differences in these key areas can serve to counterbalance each other, extreme differences can lead to severe problems.

(11) *Choose someone who is accepting of you and is not always trying to change you into someone else.* Never marry on the assumption that you or your partner will make drastic changes. If you do not feel both accepting and accepted, then proceed with caution.

(12) *Choose someone who can be supportive and understanding*

when the need arises. While self-development and independence are admirable qualities, they are much more easily obtained when your partner is supportive of your efforts and is there to lift you up if you stumble. A person who is constantly criticizing and tearing down his or her mate is laying the groundwork for the partner to develop a poor self-image and subsequently for them to build a miserable life together.

(13) *Choose someone who is determined to make marriage work.* Of all the qualities listed here, this may well be the most important. Unfortunately, many couples give up too easily, heading for the divorce courts the first time serious problems develop. This is not to say that some marriages should not be terminated; it is to reaffirm the importance of perseverance in most successful human endeavors. Love for and commitment to each other, while important, are not enough. If the marriage is to endure when the going gets rough, as it inevitably does, then perseverance, patience, and determination to make the relationship work are essential.

(14) *Insist that your partner go with you for counseling before marriage.* Premarital counseling can be helpful in spotting potential trouble areas between partners. Unfortunately, most couples never seek such assistance until after marriage. Even then they often wait until the problem has become one of major proportions or the relationship is beyond salvaging. Although the term continues to be used, much of what is today called marriage counseling could more appropriately be referred to as divorce counseling. Some counselors estimate that as many as nine out of ten couples who come to them under the guise of marriage counseling are really looking for help in separating, since one or both of the partners in the relationship has already decided that the marriage is beyond repair.

We realize that it would be impossible to find someone with all these qualities, for such a person would be nearly perfect. But each is important and should be given serious consideration in the choice of a partner for life.

conclusion

It is assumed that most couples marry because they love each other. If we interpret the marriage vows literally, we can also assume that most of these same people felt at one time that their love was strong enough to sustain them and hold them together as man and wife so long as they both should live.

Unfortunately, this is not always true. The millions of marital casualties each year demonstrate in a most dramatic way that many couples once in love have become so disenchanted with marriage to each other that they are no longer able or willing to live together.

In the hope that those contemplating marriage might be spared the tragedy of divorce, we have attempted to share some of the experiences and mistakes of couples who have themselves been casualties or victims of unhappy marriages. As a result of this sharing, we hope that individuals planning to marry will take a long and thorough look at themselves, their intended spouses, and the kind of relationship they have with each other.

It is unfortunate that many couples never do so. Because of the tendency to "put your best foot foward" while dating, many couples never really give each other the opportunity to be themselves. Consequently, they enter marriage with incomplete and one-sided pictures of their partners. Although some couples manage to continue this charade for a while, marriage, with its many responsibilities and pressures, may prove to be such a stress-provoking situation that personality traits and behavior previously played down or glossed over eventually come to the forefront.

We hope that in the preceding pages we have caused some to stop and ask themselves questions such as these: Why do I want to marry this person? Is our relationship based on healthy needs? What will life with this person be like in ten years?

If these and other questions raised in the book are answered, it is our belief that those individuals in the process of choosing a husband or wife will be in a better position to make a choice with which they can live in the years ahead.